Free MP3 downloads of the Hadji-ka Brainwave
Meditation and 7 Sets of Runes are available with
the purchase of this book. To obtain your copy of
the MP3 downloads, scan the QR code or use
this link: https://www.iampresence.com/bridge

The Bridge of
No Time

Becoming a Master of the Runes

Almine

The Secret Traditions of Rune Divination

Published by Spiritual Journeys LLC

First Edition December 2015

Copyright 2015

P.O. Box 300
Newport, Oregon 97365

US toll-free number: 1-877 552 5646

www.spiritualjourneys.com

Cover Illustration: Charles Frizzell

Almine portrait by Benno Klandt

Manufactured in the United States of America

ISBN: 978-1-941930-14-4 Softcover

ISBN: 978-1-941930-15-1 Adobe Reader

Table of Contents

The Runes of the of the Unfolding Journey

The Runes and their Story

The Symbol of the Grand Masters of the Runes

Resurrected Instruments of Infinite Intent

Additional sources of information for the Rune master:

It is highly recommended that the Rune master use the *Book of Runes*, not only for the additional information that it contains, but also for its power. The *Book of Runes* is an alchemical equation designed to act as a power object to prevent etheric interference and subliminal programming.

The breathing techniques found in *The Sacred Breaths of Arasatma*[1] are an essential tool to assist in creating the full use of the extended pranic tube that is necessary for the powerful mastery of the runes.

---

[1] See http://alminewisdom.com/collections/books/products/the-sacred-breaths-of-arasatma.

The New Expanded and Enhanced DNA Rose
Depicting the sound chambers of an evolved beings' DNA

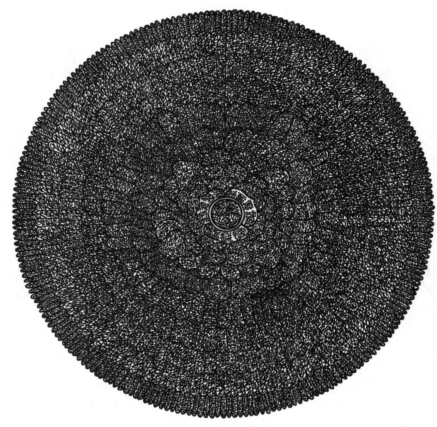

In the spring of 2014, the huge evolutionary event occurred
that awakened the capacity to utilize the inner sensory
responses to Infinite Intent: The tenth row of 672 sound
chambers within the DNA rose activated.

The Story of the Runes

The First Four Sets of Runes

In 2012, I was asked by one of our international lecturers to prepare runes for his upcoming visit to Russia. After 10 hours of revelations, the first four sets of Runes were received. For the following year and a half they were only available in Russia.

A great deal of information had been translated during 2012 for the Russian students. The reason for this was that Russia was most at risk for the cataclysms predicted for 2012. The strategy was that through giving advanced, life-altering truths (including those found in the runes), time would be stretched. This would give us more time to create a graceful change through increased perception. On the 13th of February while our lecturers were in Moscow, an asteroid narrowly missed the Earth and a meteor (previously predicted to fall on Moscow) fell instead in a non-populated area of the Ural Mountains of Russia. 2012 was over.

The Additional Three Sets of Runes

At the beginning of the summer of 2014, an additional three sets of runes presented themselves. As I translated their meanings from the ancient glyphs, I became aware that the totality of all seven sets represented the Seven Fields of Perception, the Seven Dimensions available to man. They were the devices used to interpret messages from these fields for an individual's guidance.

The Seven Fields had been studied and accessed through the ages by means of specific disciplines: Shamanism, Incorruptible Magic, Healing with light and frequency (Belvaspata), Mysticism, Metaphysics, the study of activating Godhood and the ever-new flow of Revelation.

The 672 Runes (7 x 96) represent the inner senses of an evolved being. The art of the Rune master is to activate the senses of inner space and use their guidance for action in outer realities. The master also clears and uses the seven outer senses available to a conscious being (see the Book of Runes).

The Story of the Additional Three Sets of Runes

I traveled to the Altai region of Siberia to give a retreat to a private group. The couple (whom I had seen in many classes) living in the area and attending the retreat was Edward and his wife. During the class, I complemented him on becoming one of our most accomplished alchemists, using the tool of the Qi Vesta.

As I spoke to him, I saw a vision of him standing in a long, dark green cloak with many symbols on it. To his left, a white owl hovered in the air. The vision was powerful, but too fleeting to discern what the symbols or sigils were. For four days the vision repeated itself and at night the white owl started coming to my window. The white owl is the symbol of death and I wondered what message it was carrying.

On the fourth day, our group went to a sacred hill where an ancient stone circle and white cloths tied around tree branches, indicated that for centuries pilgrimages of prayer and devotion had been made there. I explained to the group that during resurrection, life and death combine and the serpentine energetic channels twining around the pranic tube (the Ida and Pingala) become one in a holy marriage. They exit the top of the head after this metamorphosis. To the Earth, this was the place of the merged Ida and Pingala exiting.

Edward had asked me to activate an ancient language for him and in a spontaneous ceremony with me, we spoke the ancient language of the area. I once again saw him in the cloak, but this time I could see that the symbols were the 672 runes I had received. I heard the words: Grand Master of the Runes.

The day before, one of the women in our group who was also from the area, had a massive clearing of past trauma as she lay beside the river. That evening she passed away, leaving with a cry from her mouth. No pulse or breathing remained. I saw that she could be resurrected by calling her back into a resurrected body in which the Ida and Pingala had been joined. It took about ten minutes before this was accomplished. To my great relief, she started breathing again. She abruptly sat up and said, "I was dead, but you resurrected me".

The next and last day of the retreat, I initiated Edward as a Master of the Runes, clearly seeing a gathering of Grand Masters taking place on the hill of Altai in Siberia. The owl was correct: someone did die, but was resurrected. The following day I would better understand that the Siberian traditions of the Runes was also being resurrected.

At dawn the next morning, Edward and his family drove me to the airport. I asked him what was the graveyard that I kept feeling was calling me. He explained that it was only accessible by horse or helicopter. It was discovered as a burial place where for centuries shamans had gone to die.

He told me that a mummified shaman was discovered, her body covered with runes. Much against the objections of local shamans, the body was flown to Moscow so that the glyphs could be translated. Oral traditions had said that the area would not flood as long as her body was undisturbed.

The scientist trying to translate the glyphs went mad (runes are the language of the non-cognitive realm of inner space) and the floods came. Even though she was later returned, the body had been desecrated. I thought briefly how there had been floods the day before I arrived, and that although there were floods predicted for the last day I was there, they never came. The sacred runes were of a level never before found among man, but the rune tradition was once again alive and well upon Siberian lands.

On the 16th of August 2014, the planet experienced its second resurrection – the joined Ida and Pingala were engulfed in an enlarged pranic tube. Inner and outer space would become interactive: the time of the Grand Masters of the Runes was at hand.

The Initiation of the Master

Mastering the sets of Runes 1–4

- The primary priority is to acquaint yourself with the first four sets in this manual. Study the messages and principles of set 1. Understand how the dramatic dialogues are revealing how opposites are really one.
- Practice the principles of the sets in your daily life. As the illusion of opposites release, power is made accessible to you, in order to understand the deeper meaning of the runes.
- Study and live the runes of each set as the principles are mastered. The first four sets embody the principle 'complexity within simplicity'. They are deceptively simple, with depth of meaning that can only be felt by approaching a rune non-cognitively.
- Each set with its principles and its corresponding runes, will take approximately one week of daily work to complete. Make dedicated decisions to live the principles of the runes and their concepts as given in the sets.
- After four weeks of study and preparation (assuming daily, dedicated attention is given) a Rune Master or Grand Master must be contacted in order to receive initiation. The initiating master will also be responsible for providing a certificate of initiation. *Self-initiation cannot be done.*

The Initiation of the Grand Master

Mastering sets 5–7 of the Runes

An additional three weeks of study and preparation (assuming daily, dedicated attention is given) is required for Grand Master level initiation. A Rune Grand Master must be contacted in order to receive initiation in person. The initiating master will also be responsible for providing a certificate of initiation. *Self-initiation cannot be done.*

Rune Initiations Guidelines

- Self-initiation cannot be done for Master or Grand Master level.
- Master level initiation may be done long-distance.
- Grand Master level initiation must be done in person, in the physical presence of the initiating Grand Master.
- Master and Grand Master initiations can be done with no waiting period between levels, with completion of the required study for each level.
- Initiations can be performed up to, and including, your own level of initiation. Grand Masters can initiate both levels, Masters can initiate only Master level.

The Initiation: The Sacred Agreement

- *Chavech herseta anech usatva menenush selsavach uresbi kelenush. Estre uskavi serseta manuvesh eklet huresbi skavavi. Selsach neshtu privahas etrusvavi sihut aleskla manu.*

  Fearlessly the Master (Menenush) walks between the worlds of life and death, for both are as one to the resurrected being. To live from the divinity within will be my highest aim.

  (The Master asks the initiate if he agrees. Proceed when the initiate answers yes.)

- *Skararech ereste blivabat arestu visprachvi seranut hersatu mines. Kashta nensut arares vibrech usetvi el eshata vibrechvi. Suhut menenush kelavespi arsat mananu ures harastavi.*

  A life of dedication to the journey of discovery of the sacred essence of all life. I am an explorer of consciousness, a pioneer of the unknowable. As Rune Master (Suhut Menenesh), I am a bringer of guidance and light.

  (The Master asks the initiate if the initiate agrees and proceeds if so.)

- *Skre uhus estechvi prihas usut menhur karares velstrut manavesh. Skelehur sterut asakla plibaranes trevesur krivavespi mesetuch ares usatva usprinanes elestu. Suhut menenesh kavanes klihastra bihanat kelestre skravavet ekletvi urasta.*

  I am the speaker of the ancient language of the inner realms. A bridge of communication between the known and the unknown mysteries of existence. As Master of the Runes, I am a beacon of luminosity to uplift the hearts of man.

  (The Master asks the initiate if the initiate agrees and proceeds if so.)

- *Elsur anet priha. Eskrutvi misach herestu viresbi usatve misetu kalanas husbe. Skarsaba sekretu viras ares esatu plihesva*

ukranesvi araras. Saranut krives uherenustra serchsetu.
Karechpaha nesetu arak persava nenes ustre kiranech serekveratu.
From the beginning of time an agreement has been made that those will arise who bring peace to the land. In my heart let it begin, that my footsteps might bring harmony to all lands.
(The Master asks the initiate if the initiate agrees and proceeds if so.)

I now initiate you with the first four sigils of Master of the Runes.

Note: For the Grand Master level the initiation agreement is the same except the above statement becomes, "I now initiate you with the last three sigils of Grand Master of the Runes".

The Four Sigils for the Initiation of the Master of the Runes

The sigils are to be drawn (signed) over the areas of the body as indicated while saying their names.

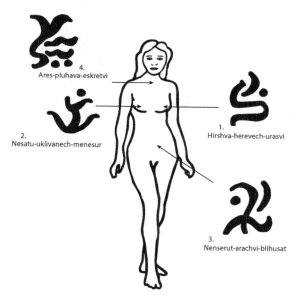

Sigil names

1. Left nipple: **Hirshva-herevech-urasvi**

2. Right nipple: **Nesatu-uklivanech-menesur**

3. Navel: **Nenserut-arachvi-blihusat**

4. Sternal notch (indentation at bottom of throat):
    Ares-pluhava-eskretvi

Close with the words:
Esaru michve huranes uvasvi.

In harmony with unfolding life, as Master of the Runes may you walk with reverence, as a blessing to all life.

The Three Sigils for the Initiation of the Grand Master of the Runes

The sigils are to be drawn (signed) over the areas of the body as indicated while saying their names.

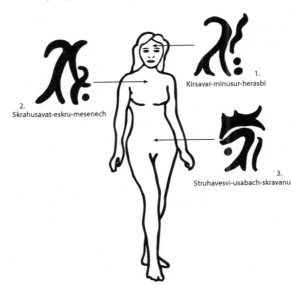

Sigil names

1. Forehead (between eyebrows): **Kirsavar-minusur-herasbi**

2. Sternum: **Skrahusavat-eskru-mesenech**

3. Navel: **Struhavesvi-usabach-skravanu**

Close with the words:
Urasvi herashtu menachvi selevit-sklura perusvi.

I am a bridge between the one and the many. To the Infinite, the glory forever and ever.

The Meditation

After the initiation the master is asked to meditate (using the music of the *Hadji-ka Brain Wave Meditation* that accompanies this book) on the turquoise chakra of the high heart. Visualize it opening like a gate beyond the speed of light, until the entire cosmos is visible through oneself as a portal.

The Seven Steps of Mastery

Step 1

Mastering the Tool of Duality

That which through dependency becomes a tyrant, through mastery becomes a tool...

~ Almine

The Field of Perception of Shamanism
The Wheel for the Runes of the Field of Shamanism

Isara unech herut arsava
Misach herevispi menevit arsata

Power through alignment with the interconnectedness of existence

The Seven Perceptions of Shamanism cultivate our acknowledgment of the interconnectedness of all life.

The Judgments of the Mind, Heart and Spirit

Value judgments of the Mind, Heart and Spirit keep us from our mastery by locking us into the powerless state of duality. The master must learn to value both poles equally in order to use opposites as a tool, emphasizing one or the other in his or her expression as suits the strategy of the master's life. This prevents the master from becoming trapped by duality. It is suggested that a day of contemplation and internalization be given to each of the pairs of opposites. Over the ten days of devoting time to this, carry the sigil of power related to the specific pair you are studying with you that day. The sigils impart subtle, non-cognitive information to the master to assist bringing resolution to their illusion of separation.

The Seven Perceptions of Shamanism

Judgments of the Mind

1. Arrogance versus Humility

    Arrogance occurs when we feel we have the power and perception to master the level of life we are experiencing. When life bumps us to the next level, we feel out of depth and humble. But when we embrace change, it comes as an effortless flow rather that the bumps that occur when we arrogantly think we know. Then wonderment at the continual revelations of the unfolding miracles of life replaces the up and down movement of arrogance alternating with humility. When humility is defined as the recognition of life as a never-ending mystery, it has no opposite. The known is like a snapshot of an instant that depicted a small part of the river, never to repeat again.

2. Captivity versus Freedom

The appearance of the opposite poles of Freedom versus Captivity disappears when we realize that what is freedom to one, is captivity to another, because as all opposites the concepts are relative and subject to individual perspectives.

When a specific level or reality is outgrown, it seems confining and constricting. Freedom is seen as the next level of evolution that we achieve. Freedom from suffering can be achieved by living in the moment. All becomes more easily endured if we are required to endure it for only a moment at a time. Suffering becomes our jail when seen against the backdrop of linear time.

3. Chaos versus Order

Chaos is the process of destructuring patterns and belief systems that hold us captive. The structure of our lives, regarded as order, is upheld by mind. Chaos loosens the grip of mind, thereby enabling the brilliance of effortless knowing that ensues from the silencing of the dialogue of the mind.

Chaos becomes disruptive only when it is called upon to facilitate forced change. Change gracefully unfolds when it comes unresisted. The illusion of order is like a snapshot taken of the river as it flows. We cannot know it by its image because it is like life, new every moment. The interaction of chaos and order is merely the conversion of unarticulated possibilities into expression.

The Judgments of the Mind

Sigil for Eliminating the Illusion of the Known

The Judgments of the Mind

Wheel 1
Arrogance versus Humility

Wheel 2
Captivity versus Freedom

Wheel 3
Chaos versus Order

Chavarech herstu minavi harsatnu blihavech
Erase now the blindness of constricted vision

Mespa erut harsata kuhanech sersatu uvanech
From clarity of mind comes the empowered journey

The Judgments of the Heart

1. Sadness versus Joy

   To deny sadness is to deny compassion. Sadness carves the hollows in the soul that enable us to feel more empathy and compassionate understanding. It signals the desire to change, providing the impetus to drive us beyond existing paradigms. Joy follows as a stabilizing influence. Each of these opposites is the result of judgmental occlusions that cause only partial perspectives. Temporary occlusions shape our perspective and hence our experiences.

2. Partnership versus Self-contained Aloneness

   Successful self-contained aloneness is also the key to successful togetherness.

   Self-containment comes from the integrated and supported expression of the sub-personalities. The tendency to over-polarize into inner space can be counteracted by partnership that energizes and stimulates a variety of emotions, such as fun or play. Aloneness allows us to focus on a love affair with life and with ourselves.

3. Valuing Family over Strangers

   The tendency to value the known over the unknown has been the primary cause of the trapping of awareness, and stagnation through complacency. Family, no matter how dysfunctional, is given more value because of the predictability of the interactions. They are seen as part of the individual's comfort zone and for many, as part of their identity. Because the tribe assigns labels, roles and value to its members, they provide mirrors of uniformity. Tribalism and uniformity prevent the fostering of individuality and greatness. New perception, yielding new power can come through insights of width – the lessons we gain from unknown strangers that we encounter, or for the aware from seeing deeply into family members and finding the unknown within the familiar. Both have equal value.

The Judgments of the Heart

Sigil for Eliminating the Illusion of the Unknown

The Judgments of the Heart

Wheel 1
Sadness versus Joy

Wheel 2
Partnership versus
Self-contained Aloneness

Wheel 3
Valuing Family over Strangers

Sihach elesklu haruhat mistavech usatvi
Sever now the ties of the heart that bind

Serech vavi eresut haranes esklat vavi haruness
In mastery from the tyranny of the heart I am free

The Judgments of the Spirit

1. Time versus Timelessness

    Timelessness is seen as something valuable to aspire to when time is regarded as a tyrant. As with all opposites, one cannot be more valuable than the other. Time is fluid and subjective and can seem to pass quickly or slowly. Even for one who has not mastered time as a tool, time can frequently stand still.

    The value of time as a common, coordinating reference point that everyone can relate to changed through dependency from a tool to a tyrant.

    Time is the movement of awareness in a specific space. This specific movement, or frequency, serves the useful purpose of defining space.

2. Authentic versus Unauthentic

    We can only know a quality found in another if we have at some time expressed that same quality. To be able to know the unauthentic, we must therefore have expressed unauthenticity ourselves.

    The unauthentic stems from occlusions in our vision. These constrictions of perception are deliberately held because they give us the unique perspective that differentiates one individuation from another. Our gift to Infinite Life is our unique perspective. When it is time for it to change, we release these constrictions and the specific areas of unauthenticity become authentic in their expression.

3. Conflict versus Peace

    All opposites have a mutual gift to give one another – saving its opposite from itself. The danger of peace is that unless the inner adventure of self-discovery is pursued it could lead to complacency and stagnation. Peace with loved ones and associates often comes at the cost of authentic self-expression.

Peace or conflict is a chosen response. Unacceptable behavior must be assessed in order to determine your response.

- Negative resistance: Allow the opposition to move through you because you have determined that you have already gained the insights.
- Neutral resistance: Absorb and process within that which you wish to change without.
- Positive resistance: Positive resistance remembers that you strengthen what you oppose but wishes to firmly establish a boundary, get a point across, or disabuse others' notion that you are predictable.

4. Fear versus Contentment

We are in contentment when we are at one with the flow of unfolding life. But the direction of life's flow may be the mediocre result of the masses' thoughts and feelings: the affect of the status quo. It may require the fear-inducing step of going against the flow in order to take control of the direction of our lives.

Fear is a helpful tool in that it indicates areas of existence that we have not embraced in trust and inclusive, compassionate understanding.

Fear ties up resources because it constricts the flow of power, energy and life force. In this role it serves as a capacitor or storage place for resources. When these resources are needed for transcending a present reality, the overcoming of this fear provides an abundant supply.

The Judgments of the Spirit

Sigil for Eliminating the Illusion of the Unknowable

The Judgments of the Spirit

Wheel 1
Time versus Timelessness

Wheel 2
Authentic versus Unauthentic

Wheel 3
Conflict versus Peace

Wheel 4
Fear versus Contentment

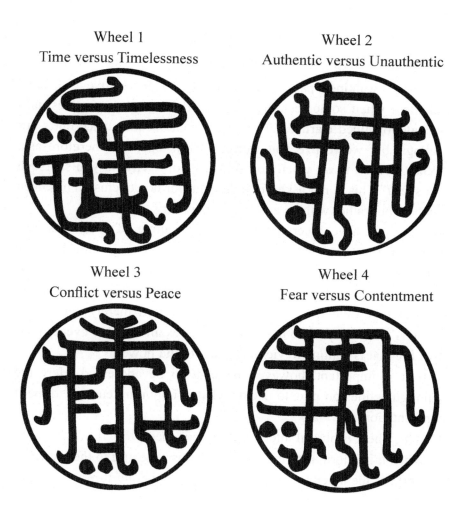

Virskla eres mivechva hersutat ekletvi manusach ares
Wherever I am is the center of holiness in my reality

Conflict Resolution

Excerpt from *Journey to the Heart of God*

Preliminary Steps in Determining Whether Conflict exists

If one is walking a path of impeccability, it is imperative to suspend judgment when some seeming offense or disagreement occurs until we have obtained clarity. For example, some acquaintance hurts our feelings, but we realize that words can mislead. We therefore ask, "What did you mean when you said ...?" or "Why do you say such and such?" This is not asked in judgment, for no conclusion has been reached, but rather with an attitude of neutrality.

When we have ascertained the true meaning of what was said through feeling the intent behind the words and getting as much clarity as possible, we can proceed. Does it still bring our hackles up or create a knee-jerk reaction? If it does, we need to ask whether it is important enough to resolve with the other person or is it merely one of our 'buttons' that was pushed in order for us to examine some event in our own life that is waiting to yield its insights and power.

If it is important, however, it needs to be addressed. Here are some guidelines on how to decide what is important enough to merit confrontation:

- When there is hurtful intent or destructiveness;
- When it is injurious to the inner child, disrespectful to the sacred world of the inner sage or belittling to the inner nurturer;
- When it violates our privacy or our sacred space;
- When it violates our mutual agreement or trust or is dishonest in any way;
- When it belittles us or suppresses expressing our individuality or causes us to have to be less than we are;
- When it attempts to manipulate, control or dominate us;

- When it criticizes or accuses us.

If it fits into one of the above or a similar scenario, the following approach should be used:
- First of all some basics should be agreed upon and perhaps even written;
- Within our relationships all feelings are valid (meaning we do not criticize someone for feeling a certain way);
- All emotions should find a safe place for expression;
- Phrases such as "You always", "You never" and "Why do you?" (when the latter is not a question but a disguised accusation) should be prohibited;
- Neither words nor emotions should be used to attack or manipulate;
- When someone is in the grip of uncontrollable rage, there should be pre-existing coping mechanisms established. They are to wash their face and hands and engage in strenuous activity (exercise bike, jogging, etc.) to organize their thoughts before expressing them;
- Writing letters that are not dispatched is also a productive form of communication where there are rage issues.

Feelings must be expressed and a solution proposed by the confronting person. This may have to be done a few times before achieving results. "When you do this, I feel this. Is it possible that in future we can try such and such?"

The appropriate way for the other person to respond is to first make sure they understand. "Are you saying that …?" If they acknowledge that a change in behavior is appropriate, it is advisable to create a backup plan since deep-seated habits are hard to break. "Can we have a secret hand gesture or phrase to remind you when old habits creep in?" or, "Could I pull you aside to remind you?"

If instead the other person starts venting, sit absolutely still and let it run its course until it is spent. Then repeat what you said, always bringing the conversation back to the relevant point. If this does not work, write it out and request a written response within a few days. If this fails to resolve the issue, the four steps of conflict resolution, discussed later are introduced (in writing if needed).

Should the disagreement persist, there are only three choices remaining:

1. **Evaluate** whether what you have in common contributes sufficiently to your life for you to continue to put up with the differences. If the differences are more significant, either sever the relationship or be prepared for ongoing discomfort.

2. **Flow** around the obstacles because the relationship has been determined to be worth saving. Be creative. He embarrasses you in public? Create a private world for your interaction and make as many public appearances as possible alone. It is never a good idea to force round pegs into square holes.

3. **Change** your attitude. Even if you do the damage control suggested in point 2, there are still going to be odd times when the offensive behavior will happen. Lift yourself above the situation like the eagle that flies above the world. Envision yourself sitting in an insulating bubble of pinkish-purple light, holding your inner child and talking to it during the occurrence.

It is never to the benefit of indwelling life to accept the unacceptable. It is also eroding to have many 'little' occurrences happen day in and day out. How diligently is the person working on improving him or herself? All these factors must be taken into consideration in coming to a final conclusion. Another helpful tool is to picture enduring this behavior for the next ten years and weigh it against the positive aspects of the relationship.

Conflict Resolution According to the Cosmic Blueprint

Excerpt from *Journey to the Heart of God*

As said earlier, it is in the densest levels of Creation where all new knowledge is gained and where life bursts forth in the most astonishing array of diversity in order to maximize the opportunity to successfully fulfill the destiny of all life forms and to explore the unknown.

But man is unique among these life forms, inspiring in other races of the cosmos both hope and fear. For man, although steeped in illusion, has the almost unfathomable ability to directly shape the unfoldment of the plan of Creation and within our DNA lies the key to initiate the in-breath of God; to take the cosmos over the edge of Creation from the 'red road' leading away from the heart of God to the 'blue road' that returns.

In order to be the way-showers for the cosmos, we have been created to represent all kingdoms and races and are a synthesis of all that is within Creation. But because Creation is a mirror of the face of God and we are representative of all Creation, we are that which most fully represents the Infinite. It is as though we hold a large piece of mirror in which the Infinite observes itself, while other creations hold much smaller fragments that reflect smaller portions of the image.

But it is also the sacred duty of man to solve all conflicts that have not yet been brought to resolution. In this way we not only evolve awareness, but as the microcosm of the macrocosm, we upload our gained insights directly to the Primary Trinity (the I AM). As a result of this increased perception, the Primary Trinity reflects down to the Creative Trinity (the Creator) an altered message as to what needs to be explored through Creation. The Creative Trinity then injects into the higher aspects of Creation (the Trinity of In-Dwelling Life or higher self) a change in the way the purpose of the Infinite must unfold. The Trinity of Materialization consequently changes the way life is shaped within materialization. And in this way man's insights have changed all that is.

But because we are representative of the whole, the divine blueprints of the large picture can also be found underlying all situations of our life, from the most mundane to the seemingly chaotic. Conflict resolution is no different; it mirrors the evolving of awareness through the four Trinities of all that is. It moves from conflict to evolved awareness through the same four distinct stages displayed in the large picture.

The Four Stages of Conflict Resolution

Stage 1

In the Primary Trinity, the I AM gathers all that is uploaded to it from the insights of our lives, all new information about the mystery of beingness. But within the Infinite the same poles attract and within Creation opposite poles attract. The Primary Trinity therefore attracts all that resonates the same. In other words, it keeps and grows more luminous from that which it recognizes to be the same, namely that which is life-enhancing. The rest is passed on to the Creative Trinity for resolution.

In the first stage of resolution, we find our common ground. Unless this is first identified, we cannot properly determine which parts to resolve in Stage 2. Failure to determine what we have in common with the opposition robs us of the priceless gift of becoming more knowledgeable by learning new aspects and viewpoints of that which we are (common ground). Too often, opponents prematurely focus on the differences during this first stage instead of simply assimilating the commonalities so that these initial gifts of insight can be received.

Stage 2

The Creative Trinity, having received all parts the I AM did not recognize as resonating similarly, now engages in analysis, weighing the unknown pieces against all that has been previously known. Once again it gathers to itself all that can be found to be the same (life-enhancing), examines it in a larger context and isolates that which is different. It now tackles the solving of these unknown pieces through externalizing them through Creation.

In this stage of conflict resolution a closer scrutiny of what is the same and what is different must take place. Those unknown pieces must be examined in depth rather than taken at face value to extract common elements. It is necessary to examine these details in the context of the larger picture. Although we may have superficial differences, are we exploring a similar pattern? Are the core issues the same even though our method of dealing with them might be different? In this way the true differences to resolve are isolated from the similarities.

The last step is to creatively externalize them. Design a case scenario – objectively examine the issues as though they are happening to someone else. Reverse roles, honestly examining what it would be like to be in the other person's shoes.

Stage 3

Within the Trinity of Indwelling Life, opposites attract. The known (light) no longer pushes the unknown away, but instead desires to incorporate it within. It wants to turn the unknown into the known through experience. For this it needs form and so must create materialization.

In conflict resolution this stage requires that we abandon our preoccupation with our own viewpoint and genuinely try to understand the opposing position. The need now arises to create a situation to test the validity of the opposing viewpoint: to see and understand it better by observing it in action. Where the stakes are high, the testing of the unknown can be done in multiple, smaller controlled settings.

Your teenager wants to date. You feel she's too young, she feels you're ruining her life because all her friends date. After completing the previous steps, one or two controlled situations could be tested wherein she is dropped off and picked up by you and has to call you if she changes locations. This option is opposed to one requiring an absolute yes or no with one party or the other feeling unheard. An informed conclusion can then be drawn as to what can be supported.

Stage 4

In the Trinity of Materialization, the unknown is incorporated into the known through experience. The previously unknown parts of the Infinite's being become known through our experiencing them and taking the time to gain the insights those experiences yield. New knowledge is gained.

In this stage we agree to disagree. The level of interaction is determined by what can be assimilated without being destructive to inner life or without being light and growth repressive. The key element of the success of this stage is to keep supporting the areas of common ground and the growth of all. Examples of the different degrees of interaction that could be allowed are:

- The in-laws don't like you, but they love your wife. Because they show their dislike when around you, you needn't be in their presence often but nevertheless support your spouse being with them as she chooses. If their intent is destructive, such as to break up the marriage, this needs to be clearly identified and the interaction must then be very minimal or terminated depending on the accompanying level of risk;
- If differences are only superficial but the common goals and philosophies are strong, we find we can live closely together or work together while honoring and supporting our diversity within our unity.

As we have moved through these stages, we have encountered the following ways of relating to each other:

- **Uniformity** – this is the stage of dependence on sameness to understand ourselves more fully.
- **Exploring sameness vs. difference** – co-dependence is experienced as we find sameness in the differences. We understand ourselves by observing that which we are not.

- **Exploring differences** – we seek our independence by focusing on that which we are not as mirrored by the other party. We determine whether the relationship is worth proceeding with.
- **Unity within diversity** – this is the stage of inter-dependence where we cooperate for the good of the common goals, supporting the diversity each contributes.

This final stage is the goal of all life since it provides the greatest opportunity for growth, whereas uniformity slows growth through stagnation. The more differences there are, the more uncomfortable the relationship will be; the greater the commitment to the greater goal, the more stable.

Relationship Types that Ensnare

The Clown

The traditions of the Norse people had Loki as the trickster. In Native American traditions he is called Hay-ho-ka, the sacred clown. In the tarot, it is the jester. The game of this personality type has the subtle agenda to keep you off balance and thus keep them in control. They are like a loose cannon – you never know where you will be embarrassed or shocked or defensive next. They pride themselves in their 'honesty' and their 'spontaneity' but their indiscriminate, undisciplined speech is designed to attract attention through startling us.

Shock and surprise causes a loss of power and energy. The Earth's cataclysms have almost always resulted in a fall of consciousness, since consciousness requires energy and an accumulation of personal power to sustain it.

People with this personality profile suck the energy up by being the center of your attention as you release resources by being taken by surprise.

The Juggler

The dynamics are the same as for the Clown in that as you focus on their games, your surprise and shock release resources they benefit from. They are the ones who imbalance you through unpredictable mood swings and rages.

There is little rationale for the sudden outbursts and the roller-coaster ride of their emotions. This instability makes it impossible to see the tantrums or rages coming, thus we are taken by surprise and drained by the experience.

The shock becomes all the more devastating because their need to keep you from abandoning them due to their rages, drives them into being particularly caring and giving in between the periods of abusiveness. We believe the latter to be their 'real' self and the rages something they can overcome. Because we open up to them during their loving, ingratiating periods, the rage causes an even greater shock, allowing them to suck up even more power and energy.

Neither part of their conduct is 'real' in that they do not represent who they could be if they lived authentically from their core, since both parts are based on controlling your responses to them.

People who are over-polarized into the masculine or feminine, are particularly prone to this unstable behavior because they are not supported by a firm foundation; their own inner feminine or masculine components. They fluctuate between self-importance and self-pity, whereas the clown has mostly self-importance, the thief operates from self-pity.

The Thief

The thief is subversive and never openly engages you. They come across as helpful, friendly and caring. They have their own way of getting your attention so that they can be empowered. They are masters at benefitting from the law that we empower what we focus on.

The range of behavior with this and the other personalities varies widely from the subtle to the more obvious and overt: at the subtle end is the ignorance and helplessness act. You explain something simple and even though they understand, multiple questions follow to hook your attention. If you do not pay your 'dues' by engaging in their game, it is done incorrectly because you 'did not explain it properly'. This personality type wants to stay connected with you at any cost; after all they have deliberately chosen you for your high ability to be their power source. They forget an item in your car or house so that you have to mail or bring it to them – more attention extracted from you.

The slightly more aggressive thief will provide you with competent assistance. In fact they will create within you, a deliberate dependency on them by doing more and more for you. Because they are rooted in self-pity, they do not feel lovable and instead settle for being needed. Many healers and psychics fit in this category. They are invigorated by the passion and fullness of another's life.

The fact that they have so little (power, success, recognition, money, popularity, etc.) and you have so much eventually causes behind-your-back destructiveness. They talk about you to others that are eager to hear, or put you in an unfavorable light, creating an even larger number of eager ears. They eventually undermine your business, reputation and finances.

The personality of the thief is based on the very first stage of social evolution, the dependency of the infant or child. This develops due to insufficient parenting. The juggler often experiences alcoholic or fighting parents. They feel uncomfortable in situations without the high tension of conflict, having become addicted to stress. They create stress and then feel angry that they are stressed. They also use stress as an excuse for their anger. They are co-dependent and follow its high-tension journey of stress that repeats over and over again:

1. I love and support you.
2. Because of how much I give, I am privileged so I can control you.
3. If you don't meet my expectations, I am furious.

The clown is independent. Its spinning and rolling tube torus is exuding a centrifugal force that pushes anything that is trying to connect with it away. If one tries to interact from the heart in an authentic way, they throw up a wall with an inappropriate response that sends you reeling.

The integrated person acts from interdependency – the low tension, high productivity stage in which people come together based on a

44

common vision, instead of needs based on deficiencies. This stage supports individual expression and honors voluntary agreements of mutual contribution with the understanding that if it no longer makes someone's heart sing to be part of it, they are joyfully released from participating. This relationship is based on voluntary roles, rather than imprisoning dependencies.

The Trout

The trout swims upstream. If everyone is gathered together to create a holy ceremony, the trout will disrupt it. They argue when there is agreement and attract attention by swimming against the intent of the group.

The trout is not a team player and in singling themselves out, they get the attention of the many. We empower what we focus on. This becomes an addictive habit by the trout, in that there is always a 'fix' of energy and resources coming his or her way that reinforces their tendency to do antisocial and disruptive things.

The Seven Perceptions of Shamanism

1. Good and Evil

To the masses the Seer spoke. As the words were heard, their bondage broke. The chains of the ages fell away. The path of freedom before them lay.

In reverent silence the people stood, to learn what was evil and what was good.

~ "Good and evil are two sides of one face, by the judgments of man, kept in place. The more explanations arise of what is good, the more the nature of evil is misunderstood."

"But Master, those whose lives are by evil consumed, to others bring hardship and pain and ruin. Is it not preferable to do good deeds? Do we not reap what we sow as seeds?"

~ "Of karma you speak, but this you must know: It is only beliefs that make it so. When at last the innocence of life you come to see, the yoke of karma shall no longer be."

"When an eternal perspective guides your eyes, they shall no longer be blinded by judgment's lies. Then shall the matrix that you have formed melt away, and freedom be born."

A silence fell over those came to hear, as the Seer's words at last became clear. Some bowed their heads, and some shed a tear as they saw the prisons they had fashioned from fear.

~ "The matrices formed from beliefs and from fear, as a cocoon to the eyes of a poet they appear. It is here where the caterpillar turns into a butterfly. Though earthbound he was, now he takes to the sky."

"What of beings of shadow that control us by fright?"

~ "The shadow you see is cast by your light. Find the blindness that lurks in your mind and gone are the shadows that haunt humankind."

"For what purpose did evil form? Was it too of our illusion born?"

~ "To know of evil, light you must understand. It is accumulated knowledge – the addiction of man. For in his compulsion to think he knows, he opposes change and won't let go."

"He shuns the unknown that comes his way. Then he opposes graceful change. A life of surrender gently unfolds. But when resisted, it into a tyrant grows."

"Thus the belief systems that around the known arise are from man's opposition to the unknown derived."

"About evil, so that we its insights may gain, what is its nature? Please explain."

~ "It comes as forced change, cloaked in pain. Life from one form to another must make way. Fluidly forming, no pattern stays the same. When we embrace structure that we know, we call it good though it obstructs the flow. When forced change comes to set it free, the destructuring is called bad by humanity."

A thoughtful silence upon them lay, as they contemplated the words the Seer did say.

At last the silence was broken by a young child's voice: "If there is no good or evil, what determines our choice?"

~ "With the eyes of a child that only innocence can see, the master must walk in humility. Yet with awareness of where his heart leads, he follows the path of inevitability."

"When the clamor of the mind is stilled and the heart's needs self-fulfilled, the highest choice stands revealed. To this the enlightened one must yield. When the high road beckons we cannot resist. In reality then, a choice does not exist."

"What would happen Master, if what we know could stay?"

~ "The river of unfolding life would wither away."

2. Simplicity and Complexity

"Master, does holiness in simplicity lie? Releasing worldly attachments and of material goods deprived? Is it not then that oneness with the Infinite we can find?"

~ "How can withdrawing from everyday life bring oneness when it is an act of exclusivity? Holiness lies in the heart of simplicity, but so too in complexity. The presence of the Infinite is everywhere to be found. Even in the crowded street does it abound."

"But is it not easier to feel the Infinite presence in the silent temple's simplicity?"

~ "The bodily temple of a surrendered life is a place of sanctity. As materialism stalks the one engrossed in complexity, so too does complacency haunt the one in simplicity."

"Then how shall we know which life to choose? What measure to know what is best shall we use?"

~ "When opposites are deemed by mind as far apart, their oneness is still known to the wisdom of the heart. There is no need to choose when within one the other resides, when in the heart of complexity, simplicity abides."

"How does this in our lives apply? How can we see beyond duality's lies?"

~ "In simplicity great awareness can be found of the intricate details that in complexity abound. In overwhelming complexity the mind grows still. Unable to cope, it surrenders its will. Time compresses in the moment simplicity is found, even in the midst of the milling crowd."

"Master, is it so that when one pole is overvalued, its opposite does grow?"

~ "Thus I have taught that you may know, that you strengthen that which you oppose."

The Seer could see that they did not know how to apply it, which way to go.

~ "From your judgments do opposites grow, in your belief systems do you make it so. In wonderment embrace that which may come. Let your open heart embrace the many within the one."

3. Freedom from Karma

"Master, how can liberation ever come when karma rules the lives of everyone?"

~ "No force exists that ever can bind the lives of any one of humankind. It is but the belief that makes it so. Karma goes when the innocence of life you come to know. "

"But, what of those who great harm bestow? Should they not reap what they sow?"

~ Then woe unto those who make it so, for now those who retribution bestow have themselves become subject to karmic revenge. Thus the cycle continues and does not end."

"When no force exists that ever can bind, then why do the laws of nature rule humankind?"

~ It seems so only because you are governed by mind. In silence of thought, miracles you'll find."

"Tell us now Master, how karma began. How did it gain control of the lives of man?"

~ "From regrets it was born: four bands of karma that the four directions form. Physical life holds the regrets of deeds. The realm of soul holds the regrets of emotional needs. The realms of spirit, of which there are two, hold regrets of that which you did not do."

"How can we transcend the regrets that we hold?"

~ "Through acknowledged perfection the heart trusts what it cannot behold. Then in complete surrender does life unfold. Without regrets, karma relinquishes its hold. As liberation comes, life in grace unfolds.

"How can we not regret the chances that are lost, deeds undone at happiness' cost?"

~ "Nothing is undone, it is not as it seems. To think something is amiss is to believe in the dream. Within duality is the law of compensation. Nothing can be gained and nothing can be taken. Within the moment is contained all that is needed within the pattern of Divine will to remain."

"But what if through blindness we from the pattern stray? What if in ignorance we walk another way?"

~ "There is no other way than Divine Intent. With grace we walk it, or with malcontent. What then could we possibly regret? That which seems wrong is but our expectations that are not met."

"How will it be when karma is released, when from the consequences of our actions at last we are free?"

~ "When karma is no more, you are no longer haunted by what was before. But when the will of the Infinite is ignored there are most definitely consequences in store. Hardship comes to show us the way when though unaware, we go astray."

The Seer could see that their hearts with doubt were filled. Thus once more the Seer spoke that their fears might be stilled:

~ "Awareness of what is meant to be when we cease to strive comes effortlessly. The Infinite's will to you is shown, through the whisperings of your heart it can be known. When you no longer try to control, the heart can hear clearly how life should unfold."

4. The Power of Attitudes

"Master, what tools of enlightenment must we cherish above all else?"

~ "Your attitudes can make of hell a heaven, or of heaven a hell. They are the sails that help you set your course. They oppose or cooperate with unfolding life's force. Through your attitudes is your power lost or reclaimed. They make a stairway of enlightenment from stumbling blocks of pain."

"Your attitudes shall determine how your life shall be, whether filled with grace or adversity. They squander or conserve your energy. They give perceptions that you may see that hardships are gifts of luminosity."

"Can life be determined by everyone? Can the way we respond shape what comes? What then of the will of the Holy One?"

~ "No slaves shall you be, but masters of your own destiny. Each one a unique lens through which the Infinite Light shines, each one a perspective of the Divine. The authentic response of an open heart, blessings to the interconnectedness of life impart. The gifts of the moment are ours to use, to turn into blessings through our attitudes."

"Which attitudes Master, shall we emphasize? Which shall we emphasize throughout our lives?"

~ "If you wish to contribute in meaningful ways to the quality of the unfoldment of every day, the attitudes with your life you must embrace are love, gratitude and heartfelt praise."

"Of these three, which is the easiest to assist mastery?"

~ "In corporeal life, gratitude comes easily. Love comes to those who to death succumb, and praise is natural to an ascended one. Gratitude cannot only be for what to us desirable seems. Even when it breaks our heart, in the cosmic plan it plays a part."

"Master, what does gratitude bestow on one who for everything gratitude knows?"

~ "Gratitude brings increase of that which inspires its birth."

"But will it not also through our gratitude increase hardship on Earth?"

A murmur of approval rippled through the crowd. That one of them would question deeply, they were sincerely proud.

~ "It is not hardship that should inspire gratitude, for this is the attitude of a slave in servitude who must accept all that comes as good. Instead, it is the opportunity to demonstrate your mastery. To show the trust you feel in the grander scheme that to us is unrevealed. Through gratitude in pain much is gained: Opportunities awake that dormant have lain."

"What about love, Master?" a poet wanted to know. "But one word describes what itself in different ways show."

~ "The horizon is different when from a mountaintop seen. It varies as well for one on the ground and one in the top of a tree. So too different forms of love, depending on consciousness, are revealed. The potency of earthly love awakens in one's being the ability to truly know what inclusivity means."

"In the stages of love's progression, we arrive at divine compassion. Then great rapture can be felt as we acknowledge everything as the self."

"Is this for the one who in expansion and bliss abides?"

~ "Beyond this seasonless condition, the love affair with life does lie. In life's eternal journey never does one arrive."

From the back of the crowd a voice was raised: "Tell us Master, what of praise?"

~ "Praise is a focus chosen by some. It is the liberation from drudgery for everyone. It is that which sees above the storm and that from which the eternal perspective is born. It does not see the strife that around us lies, but focuses on the grandeur of the starry skies."

"It does not disacknowledge humanity's cries, but sees the perfection that behind the appearances lies. A master of praise will fully engage in the toil and the strife of every day life. But with lightness of heart he will play his part."

"As the song of praise sings through his cells, he blesses all life and himself as well."

5. Emptiness and Fullness

Then asked a monk who for emptiness strives:

"Tell us Master, of emptiness of the mind."

~ "Do not seek to find emptiness within the silence of the mind. Within the emptiness of mind, the fullness of effortless knowing resides. The birthplace of genius beyond thinking lies.

"Thoughts are released when opposition to life will cease. The miracles you seek then will increase. When boundaries are no longer enforced by thoughts, a life beyond mortal boundaries becomes yours."

"But is not the emptiness the condition we need from the cycles of life and death to be free? Do our attachments not enslave and bind, the attachments formed by the heart and mind?"

~ "There are many roads that up the mountain lead. There are many ways from the tyranny of mind to be free. Many the ways the silence of the mind can be achieved. As it is emptied, the fullness of effortless knowing can be achieved."

"Tell us other ways Master, please. What lies beyond the way of a priest? Tell us too, which way is best for the busy householder for whom there is no rest?"

~ "Every day opportunities are brought that would yield perceptions when they are sought. Belief systems abdicate their tyrannical reign when confounded by the insights you have gained. At last, as perception stretches beyond beliefs, the dictatorship of mind must concede defeat. Thus it must bow down in silent humility before the unknowable journey throughout eternity."

The crowd stood in thoughtfulness. Then one asked, "In this way, where is the bliss?"

~ "Bliss is the trap and enchantment of silencing the mind through emptiness. Addiction could also come from perception, from the rapture that the surges of power bring. If succumbing to the temptation to stay in these stages persists, the master's power for further evolution will no longer exist."

"Master, you have taught us that perception does more power yield. Although I can understand that succumbing to bliss forms a stagnant field, how then does perception eventually our power deplete?"

~ "Shun not the perception, but the addiction to the rapture it will produce. For effortless knowing both methods must be used. The simultaneous expression of opposites, individuated through emphases alone, is the way of life we seek to make our own."

"In this way you become the observer and the observed at once, fully engaged! Addiction only comes from abandoning life's stage. Become not only the spectator, but also the actor in the play. This combines the outer world with the direction of within. At this point your mastery of circumstances begins."

"Why did our religions not tell us of these truths?"

~ "Because they have forgotten that they are but a finger pointing at the moon. With greed they wish to hold you, not have you gone too soon. They represent a part of the road you are merely passing through."

"What purpose do they serve, religions known before? Are they the platform from which greatness is born?"

~ "The moment is the birthplace of all you can possibly be. The past ever changes by living moments gloriously. The moment is the source of life; do not look at what has been. Through surrender life renews and changes effortlessly.

6. What is Truth

"That which is holy to one, to another is not so. When both deliver their highest thought, how are we to know?"

~ "It is not truth, but wisdom they impart when it comes from learning rather than from the heart. To understand the meaning of truth is the place to start."

"But Master, groups have formed around principles of the mind."

~ "Choosing greatness over mediocrity, you must leave the tribe behind.

"Is solitude then the answer to finding truth within?"

~ "Not solitude, but self-sovereignty is where greatness begins. The tribe promises approval, which puts you in their debt. The price to pay is conformity, thus it delivers bondage instead."

Solemnity engulfed the crowd as they pondered what was said. Was detachment in the name of truth what the master meant?

~ "Do not be dismayed, nor forsake the roles you play. The heart is only free when you express authentically. Neither uniformity nor diversity serves your loved ones beneficially. Children in uniformity raised will have their minds enslaved. Within the unity of unconditional love, support the individual diversity of their thoughts."

"Is truth then arbitrarily formed within an individual's soul? Does no set standard ever exist that truth for all be known?"

Before the Master's answer came another's voice was raised. "Master, tell us please why similar traits are cherished in diverse societies? Some valued beliefs that seem inherent to man, somewhere in some common root began."

~ "The discomfort that arises when the fluid nature of truth is seen comes from not understanding that today's truth is not the same as what has been. The obsession to discover a truth that cannot change, feeds the world's belief systems that on your obsession prey. Where obsession and neediness linger, control will enter too. Through providing the illusion of certainty, with dogma they control you."

"Life is like a river that endlessly flows, even though an image can capture a moment as it goes. The image then to others can be shown, but it doesn't mean that the next moment the river can be known."

"The universe is unknowable even though it seems the same. To think that life can be known is arrogant and profane. The experiences of the moment that you to yourself reveal are but a fleeting glimpse before to change they yield."

"Master how shall we live with such uncertainty?"

~ "With the wonderment of a child in utmost humility. To such a one life reveals its mysteries. The doors to the unfolding secrets of life close to the one who thinks he knows. The premises of man, cherished throughout the lands, are the pillars that support a specific reality. Greatness is to transcend the one of humanity."

"Will we then not alone in our reality be, or will this be the supported diversity of which you speak?"

~ The Master nodded approvingly. "Among them yet in your own sacred reality shall you be. Test by living the premises of man until their deeper meaning you understand. All that you deem sacred and hold most dear shall drop the masks of sanctity and become more clear. Then can the old duality no longer bind you to its reality.

"What is holy and what is truth?" came the voice of the monk as the Master paused.

~ "Wherever you walk with the purity of a child is the most holy place you'll find. The moment is your sacred sanctuary in which your highest truth is an act of unbridled authenticity."

"Master," the monk did ask, "may I speak? Then truth is not something we should seek, but the authenticity we masterfully express?"

~ The Master answered, simply, "Yes!"

7. Beyond Polarity

"Master what purpose does polarity fulfill? Though we seek for oneness, why does it linger still?"

~ "When we examine aspects of life as separate we form duality. As our awareness shifts from one pole to another we create polarity. Polarity as movement is not as it seems, it is the energy source that fuels separation's dream.

"It seems that the masses live in polarity, but that the sage in his wisdom has overcome duality. Oneness must then be the evolved stage of mastery?"

~ "Oneness is the opposite of duality. When one pole is valued more than it's opposite it brings adversity. For that which is denied its right to be will rise, and challenge you virulently."

"In trying to evolve beyond the reality of opposite poles we enter oneness, but it is just another opposite pole of duality. What then Master, could we ever achieve that will help us from illusion to be free?"

~ "What is illusion but a temporary focus of the eye that sees only part, and the rest denies? It is a tool of emphases to use as you will. Master it well, that its purpose it may fulfill. As for what one can aspire to, which beyond oneness and separation lies: your existence within Infinite Life is what you will find."

"Do we achieve it when we both oneness and separation combine?

~ "That which is real is not from unreal parts comprised."

"As we see these separate realities as curtains that our vision distorts, and we thrust them aside, what is in store?"

~ "A potent existence in which you need not pay for any advantage that you gain; a life in which you grow from grace to grace, and where progression does not come from a linear pace."

"In perpetual alchemy, from a cooperative dance with Infinite Intent, explosive results occur with very little energy spent. From alchemy results are leveraged by the equation of the components. The energy source for this level of life comes from alchemical combustion."

"What are the components that interact and what makes them perpetually interact?"

~ "Perpetual alchemy has three parts that combine: the field of Infinite intent, the individual perspective, and the presence of the Divine."

"Is it the presence of Source that is the perpetual motivating force?"

~ "Of course it is so. It is the only source from which energy can perpetually flow."

"Then how can we this exalted state achieve? How can duality and oneness inseparable be?"

~ "Duality is part of external time and place. Oneness is found in your inner space. When surrendered participation in life takes place, you are starting to merge inner and outer space. The outer stimulates and the inner stirs. The more the inner senses respond in turn, the more they participate in your outer world. "

"Will this the evolved reality create one in which masterful manifestation takes place?"

~ "To try and create what already exists would be wrong. In this elevated state you have always belonged."

Using the First Four Sets of Runes for Guidance and Manifestation

Using the First Four Sets of Runes for Guidance and Manifestation

The first four sets of runes have four power wheels to strengthen the guidance and manifestation functions of the runes.

Placement of the 4 Power Wheels

- At the bottom place the *Wheel of Infinite Potential*
- On top of that place the *Wheel of the 300 Lemurian Angels* (the 300 nuances of feminine expression)
- On top of that place the *Wheel of the 300 Atlantean Angels* (the 300 nuances of masculine expression)
- At the top place the *Wheel of Perpetual Regeneration* (represents the 144 Tones of Purity or effortless Perpetual Regeneration)

Working with the Runes

There are 2 ways of working with the runes in conjunctions with the Power Wheels:

1. Divination

    a) Place the stack of Power Wheels either under your chair or below your feet as you lie down.

    b) Bring the wheels up through your body one at a time, starting with the *Wheel of Perpetual Regeneration*. Ask that they assist with clarity.

    c) If you feel that a wheel is 'stuck', breathe out any stress or constriction until it moves through.

    d) Proceed with doing a spread of your choice as described in the method for divination with the seven sets of runes.

5. Manifestation

    a) Choosing one rune or more, place it in the middle of the stack of power wheels (the stack is created as outlined above). Say a prayer of intention that the principle is emphasized in your life in the time frame that you keep the rune(s) on the stack.

    b) You may perform a longer ceremony of manifestation. For this ceremony, place the selected runes in a clockwise circle around you. Move the Power Wheels through you as previously described. When all four *Power Wheels* have moved through, voice your intention and envision how the situation will look when it fully manifests.

    c) When you are finished, pick up the runes in a counter-clockwise direction and place them in a circle around the stack of power wheels. Leave them in this position overnight if you can.

The Wheel of Perpetual Regeneration
Through Trusting Self-sovereignty

The Wheel of the 300 Atlantean Angels

The Wheel of the 300 Lemurian Angels

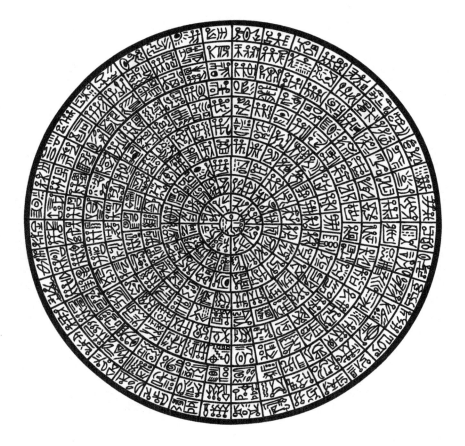

The Wheel of Infinite Potential

The Runes of the Field of Shamanism

The 96 Runes of the White Tiger

1.

Resourceful Situations

2.

Creating the Mold

3.

Vision Holder

4.

Relentless Optimism

5.

Seer's Stone

6.

Clarity of Intentions

7.

Removing Occlusions

8.

Magnificent Light

9.

Vehicle of Divine Will

10.

Impervious Sanctity

11.

Undaunted Courage

12.

Divine Sovereignty

13.

Foundation of Faith

14.

Flawless Wielder of Magic

15.

Peaceful Revolution

16.

Meticulous Consideration of Consequences

17.

Key to Ancient Bodies of Magic

18.

Unified Fields

19.

Unopened Libraries Within

20.

Sacred Secrets

21.

Reciprocal Communication

22.

Responsible Stewardship

23.

Grateful Privilege

24.

Courageous Torchbearer

25.

Eternal Perspective

26.

Thoughtful Consideration

27.

Imaginative Creativity

28.

Beacon of Light

29.

Effortless Knowing

30.

Holy Languages

31.

Sacred Symbols

32.

Graceful Dance of Life

33.

Sacred Mission

34.

Freedom through Responsibility

35.

Assignment from Mother

36.

Unity in Diversity

37.

Birthing Perception

38.

Resonant Light

39.

Exuding Light

40.

Exponential Communication

41.

Dynamic Magic

42.

Awe-inspiring Perfection

43.

Potential Revealed

44.

Building Blocks of Existence

45.

The Universal Language

46.

Mirrors of Self-Perception

47.

The Mind of the Heart

48.

Abundant Life Force

49.

Guidance from Within

50.

Co-creator with The Divine

51.

Blessings Restored

52.

**Conduit for Incorruptible
Magic**

53.

Elevated Calling

54.

Heaven on Earth

55.

Self-sustenance

56.

Vigorous Enthusiasm

57.

Revealing Luminosity

58.

Multidimensional Cooperation

59.

Marriage of Frequency and Light

60.

Enduring Love

61.

Infinite Presence

62.

Perception's Holy Spark

63.

Diligent Self-scrutiny

64.

Decisive Obedience to Heart's Guidance

65.

Mastery of White Magic

66.

Precious Knowledge

67.

Mystical Treasures

68.

Spiritual Maturity

69.

Seer of Mysteries

70.

Universal Pivot Point

71.

Spontaneous Creation

72.

Childlike Innocence

73.

Infinite Gift of Incorruptible Magic

74.

Halls of Records

75.

The Gift of Unique Perspective

76.

Discerning Sacred Value

77.

Inspiring Accomplishments

78.

Warrior against Limitation

79.

Flexible Goals

80.

Manifestation through Magic

81.

Honoring the Sacred

82.

Ancient Mystery Schools

83.

Expanding Boundaries

84.

Long-awaited Renaissance

85.

Cosmic Explorer

86.

Multi-faceted Genius

87.

Eternal Time

88.

Holding the Space

89.

Discoverer of Truth

90.

Restoring White Magic

91.

The Seat of Genius

92.

Healing Duality

93.

Evolving Physicality

94.

Embracing Information Exchange

95.

Returning to Elegant Simplicity

96.

Soothing Assurance of Victory

The Seven Steps of Mastery

Step 2

Combining the Inner and Outer Experiences of Nature to Unlock the High Heart: Portal to the Resurrected Life

In unlocking the High Heart, the figure eight formed by the cycles of life repeating cycles of inner and outer experiences becomes a Mobius strip – a journey in which the inner and outer realities become one.

Almine

The Field of Perception of Incorruptible Magic

The Wheel for the Runes of the Field of Perception of Incorruptible White Magic

Strabech Hersatu Erechba Misavech Sersatu Keretvanit

Incorruptible Magic through Cooperation with the Infinite

The Seven Perceptions of Incorruptible Magic reveal the perception hiding behind the appearances, waiting to be revealed.

Mobius Strip

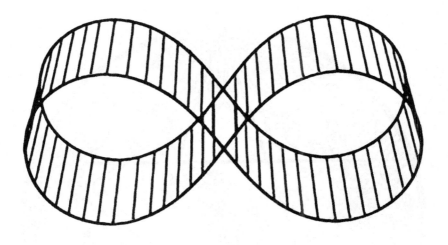

A Mobius strip is a single, continuous loop with a half twist in it.

The Seven Perceptions of White Magic

1. The Mirrors of Life

"Master," a young monk spoke with head bowed low. "How can the body know the superior wisdom of spirit and soul? How can the higher self the body's torment control?"

~ "What is the body, spirit and soul?"

The young monk looked perplexed. He did not know. In the crowd too, no one could tell. Over the crowd a silence fell.

~ "The cycles of change through which life moves are the same as what you are subject to. Life has rotated through three mirrored stages of progression: life, death and ascension."

"But Master, it speaks of the holiness of ascension in the ancient texts."

~ "Can one mirror be more holy than the next? It has always been so that when somebody knows a way beyond the cyclical journey where everyone goes, that holy he seems. But when life goes in the circle of a specific reality where one ascends to, everyone has already been. The future is the past as we've moved between the mirrors of life and death and sometimes in ascension we've been."

"Master, upon this journey through many ages as we've travelled through these stages, how must the body, soul and spirit be seen?"

~ "The vehicles that record what the experiences of these stages have been. In duality we have been caught in the trap of a mirrored life. Each mirror has vied for our attention with competitive strife. Each has promised what the other cannot give if we will but enter its domain to live."

"Then how can we trust higher self's guidance that we receive?"

~ "It will advise only so much accurately and then on important matters deceive. The body promises adventure and sensual delights, the soul promises rest and relief from physical strife. The spirit promises a heaven it dictates, a place where without emotions you may stay."

"The physical deliberately blind spots create so that physical karma, which calls you back, you will make. The soul world beckons you into death and tricks you into emotional karmic debt. The world of spirit, which ascended masters know the individual calls and through guilt controls."

Upon the faces of many was a look of dismay. Where could they find home, a safe place to stay? In trusting their soul's guidance, they felt betrayed.

"How can these mirrors come to exists? Of what do they consist?"

~ "The mirrors are what you yourself have made; from belief systems formed, tyrants they became."

"Why did we do this?" the monk asked in shame. "It brings me sadness that we are to blame."

~ "All is in perfection. Release the pain. From the fear of your vastness were they made. An incubation chamber they became. They provided your opposition so that strength you may gain."

"Without our bodies, what remains?"

~ "Your luminous and incorruptible form, when the dust of the ages is wiped away."

2. Immortality

"Master, some need to be reborn or so they claim. Some immortals do not have to die. To which must we aspire, please say."

~ "A game of mirrors do they play. Life, death and ascension are mirrors that you made. The game these masters play is to delay a specific mirror's claim."

"But is it not worthy of respect that death or life can be prolonged? Is it not a holy deed that in our sacred records belong?"

~ "All of life must be respected, whether one plays the elder or the fool. To master the game of mirrors is to become adept at the use of a tool. Whichever stage they wish to tarry cannot indefinitely be maintained. It is more of a challenge in the physical than in the soul world to stay. The physical is far more subject to the ravages of decay."

"How then should we view this, in light of what you say?"

~ "Not as an arrival point in your timeless existence, but just as a game you've played. Those who have known the rules have mastered these stages as tools, inspiring the awe of humanity instead of assisting them to be free."

"Why did the masters not the way off the treadmill show?"

~ "Because they themselves did not know."

"But if a great master could not do this after spending a life in silent bliss, how could we aspire from this journey to be free?"

~ "What is the greatest, the single mother all alone who toils for her children to make a home? Or the one who in inactivity dwells, consumed in his bliss, please tell."

Confusion stirred the crowd and they debated what to say. But then the Master answered. "Both are equally great. " At once the crowd became quiet again as for an explanation they did wait.

~ "The one who spends his days in expansion no physical karma accrues. In the game of life and death karma enforces the rules. But in stagnation that ensues when the silence of the mind in inactivity is pursued, emotional karma is accrued though invisible to you. "

"Master, you have taught us that in the soul world emotional karma must be paid. Is that why those of inactive bliss so long between rebirths can stay?"

Amazed many looked at the scholar that such a profound question did raise.

~ The master nodded earnestly, "It is as you say. The karma that was made was from deeds undone, to never feed the hungry or extend a hand to a grieving one. The purpose of his greatness was to strengthen the inner realms. Because we are all connected, this strengthened the race of men."

"And what of the single mother," asked a woman with a baby at her breast. "When does she get her rest?"

~ "With a heart that brims with love and praise, the toil of her hands turns to grace. Upon the altar of life her deeds are placed as she brings Heaven to her home's humble space. Her eyes are aglow for in her heart she knows: her reward she can find in her children's smiles."

3. Prolonging Life and Overcoming Death

"What is death and how does it occur?"

~ "Death is a purification rite that becomes necessary when we live an unexamined life. To reap the fruit of insights from the tree of our experiences is to die a little each day. This keeps death away."

"What is the cause of death's force? Where can we find its source?"

~ "In minds and hearts does death's origin start. Propelled into motion by our resistance to life and carried upon the hands of linear time."

"Please clarify Master, I cannot understand."

~ "Time arises from the resistance of man. It creates movement in the building blocks of life, the sub-atomic awareness particles unseen by eyes. In a spiraling, centrifugal motion they travel out and back again to their originating location. Thus when they return whence they began; they pummel and grind against the fields of man. This wear over the years the fields cannot bear, and so eventually crumbles and tears."

"You have said that when in trust our lives are spent, no time there is, only the moment. Please tell us if you will, does death then release its grip as time stands still?"

~ "Yes that is so, but this you must know, the spiraling rivers of awareness still from others flow. When you in your striving cease, much density do you release. Then awareness particles will move right through because they are denser than you."

"How does aging happen that ends in death? How does it come with gradual stealth?"

~ "The greatest conspiracy known to man lies not without, but within it began. The vehicles of soul and spirit did the body persuade that if soul does not occupy it, it would wither away. Death would ensue if soul withdrew, even though its place was not to occupy the body's space."

"When the physical is discouraged and hope is lost, the body's loss of soul force is the cost. The more the body loses, the more it believes it must age, a belief system by mind control kept in place."

"Speak about the soul that in the body hides, when does it its own mirror occupy?"

~ "Like a worker of stealth a disguise it needs, thus the dream body it is called and at night it leaves. Attached by a cord it returns with ease. When the cord breaks the body believes it must die and the soul leaves."

One voiced many's concern: "We are surrounded by hostility, where are we to go?"

~ "Those mirrors you created. You too can let them go by eliminating the systems of beliefs the way you do your garden's weeds. Find the origin of your deeds whether formed from beliefs or prompted by needs. Let actions flow from authenticity and freedom you will know."

"With no body, soul or spirit, what remains?"

~ " "The incorruptible matter containing all three inseparably as one. Expressing only as emphases as it has always done. Timelessly existing, hidden by illusion's veils, this luminous miracle is again revealed as they gently slip away."

4. The Evolutionary Stages of Man

"The evolutionary stages of man, explain to us the depths of the plan. What is it that they help us to gain? What is evolution's final aim?"

~ "First you must know the nature of change before you can study an evolutionary stage. Evolution is a journey around a wheel that spins. Over and over we live it until the power of its illusion dims. Then we move to another hoop, exploring again the illusions of this loop."

"Then what of progress Master? The end for which we strive?"

~ "There is no linear progression, no point at which you arrive."

"It brings discouragement when considering this, when I consider that no map of our journey exists. What then Master is the purpose of this?"

~ "Three stages of change there are as around and around you go, spiraling eternally through the unknown. It is through experience that the mystery becomes known. First there is transfiguration in which you discard the old, then you move to the next stage as on to transmutation you go. This creates higher expression from what once was law, like creating wisdom from that which you know. Then comes transfiguration to create higher capacity than before, so that more refined information in your body can be stored.

"Is man then trapped upon this wheel throughout eternity?"

~ "Three coils of three stages each lie within man's capacity. Many repetitions will he live before the next stage of eternity. For beyond the stages of man, the godhood is his destiny. Yet even there he many not tarry, ever onward he must go. Life is a journey of the unknowable, stagnation stalks us in the known."

The Stages of Change

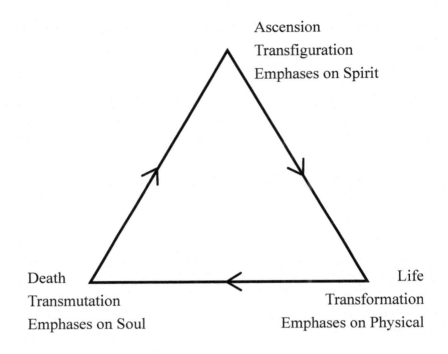

Ascension
Transfiguration
Emphases on Spirit

Death
Transmutation
Emphases on Soul

Life
Transformation
Emphases on Physical

The Evolutionary Stages of Man

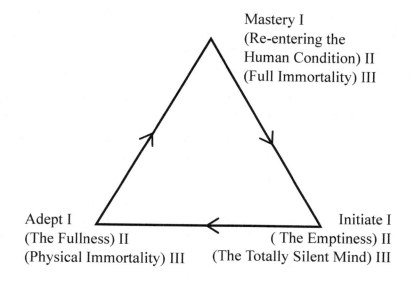

Mastery I
(Re-entering the
Human Condition) II
(Full Immortality) III

Adept I
(The Fullness) II
(Physical Immortality) III

Initiate I
(The Emptiness) II
(The Totally Silent Mind) III

"Of what are these stages comprised?"

~ "Merely a different focus of the eye. For in the stage of identity, the initiate, adept and the mastery: the perspective studies the details, life's intricacies. The next coil that the human wheel moves through is called god consciousness by you. Vast is the vision of this stage as expanded perspectives you have gained."

"What is the next large stage, is it ascended mastery?"

~ "Yes it is, and now you live both large and small perspectives simultaneously."

"If the god kingdom lies beyond, what if I cannot make the leap?"

~ "Then your journey around the wheel with more grace you must repeat."

"Is this failure? Will I be left behind?"

~ "That cannot be when you have eternal time. To the explorer who lingers, a single detail to observe, it is no failure to pause and give a flower along the way the attention it deserves."

5. What is Resurrection

"What is the way in which we transcend humanity's cycles on this journey that never ends?"

~ "A whole new reality beckons beyond, waiting for man to one day respond. The god kingdom's gateway can be breached, with transcendence it can be reached. Moving off the treadmill of time, walking among men, yet in touch with the divine.

"Can I this release through ascension find?"

~ "Leave life, death and ascension behind. Resurrection transcends leaving these stages behind. They are the stages of humanity not that which in the god kingdom you'll find."

"Will my body still be the same or will it through this process be changed?"

~ "A new energy source will be produced. For a different function will the pranic tube be used. Thus change it will, it will be larger still and a marriage between the Ida and Pingala will take place. New sub-atomic particles from the crown will be released as a gift of grace."

"What benefit will these new particles bestow? Is it a gift all mankind will know?"

~ "It changes all life not just humanity. It removes all past imprints that interfere with originality. It cleans the membrane that individuated life contains so that it free from programming remains. Else from the membrane a matrix forms and through this the bondage of life is born."

The crowd in solemnity stood, not knowing what to ask or if they should. To achieve a goal so lofty and grand was beyond what they could understand. The master sought to set their mind at ease, to release their anxiety and to restore their peace.

~ "There are steps around the wheel of humanity. Walk them well and you shall be free."

Their hearts rejoiced for they could see, how one step at a time, this could eventually be. A scholar spoke and his voice rang true: "Master to walk these steps, what shall we do?"

The Two Stages of Resurrection

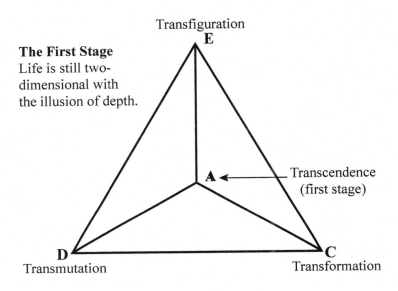

The First Stage
Life is still two-dimensional with the illusion of depth.

Transfiguration — E

Transcendence (first stage) — A

D — Transmutation

C — Transformation

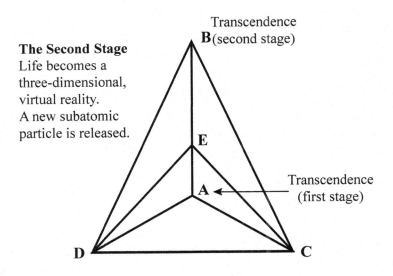

The Second Stage
Life becomes a three-dimensional, virtual reality. A new subatomic particle is released.

Transcendence B (second stage)

Transcendence (first stage) — A

E

D

C

The Transfiguration of the Pranic Tube
During Resurrection

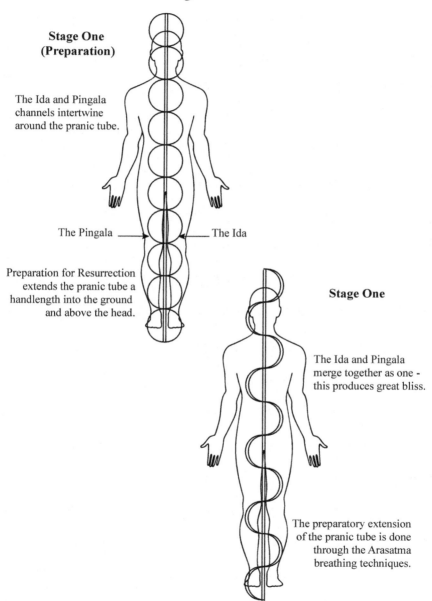

**Stage One
(Preparation)**

The Ida and Pingala
channels intertwine
around the pranic tube.

The Pingala ———   ——— The Ida

Preparation for Resurrection
extends the pranic tube a
handlength into the ground
and above the head.

Stage One

The Ida and Pingala
merge together as one -
this produces great bliss.

The preparatory extension
of the pranic tube is done
through the Arasatma
breathing techniques.

The Transfiguration of the Pranic Tube During Resurrection

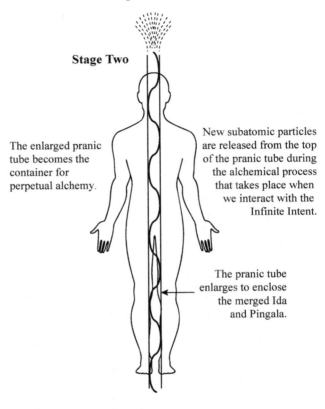

Stage Two

The enlarged pranic tube becomes the container for perpetual alchemy.

New subatomic particles are released from the top of the pranic tube during the alchemical process that takes place when we interact with the Infinite Intent.

The pranic tube enlarges to enclose the merged Ida and Pingala.

~ "A great realization you must achieve so that the illusion of the one and the many will cease to be. Opposites are they or so it seems. For their existence has always been but a dream. When you know them as veils that obscure the view of eternity, they will part and reveal the miracle of your existence within your Source effortlessly. Then are you ready to accept your divinity."

6. The Feminine and Masculine

Thus came the question from a husband and wife standing apart: "Tell us now of the affairs of the heart. Where did all the conflict start?"

~ "If the root of conflict is what you seek, it is of the inner battles we must speak. In many cultures the feminine is seen as weak, but it is from the masculine that resources leak. When social conditioning over-passivity in the feminine promotes, it stimulates the masculine into taking control. We empower what we focus on and so masculine resources drain. The feminine as the object of his focus, the energy from him gains."

The husband looked perplexed: "But she is the strident one, always controlling and vexed."

~ "Undervalued by the world, the feminine feels unheard and without a choice. When able to do so she expresses jaggedly, with harshness in her voice. Suppression brings anger that cannot be denied. With fury she releases all the tears uncried."

"Master," said the wife, "I feel so much sorrow that I cannot breathe. It is true that within I boil and seethe. Why do anger and sorrow reside in me?"

~ "The feminine seeks fulfillment from the external. She draws with a spiral of need other's energy. To the masculine like madness it seems, the spiral that she spins. Inclusive by nature, she gathers others within to support her in her neediness and thus a conflict begins."

"What will bring fulfillment? What will bring her peace? How could the feminine her eternal torment ease?"

~ "She must pursue the mystery to the edge of the unknown. Only there can the nature of the feminine truly be shown. She brings the gift of energy drawn from the mystery beyond, the unknowable beckons and with the inquisitiveness of her nature she must respond. When the external world of form becomes her chosen platform she forfeits the sovereignty of her domain. In the mystery she must journey, in the known she must not remain."

"What in the external world causes her to feel such pain?"

~ "When she seeks fulfillment from that which cannot provide, she feels a deprivation that within her heart resides. When she steps into the world of man forfeiting her rightful place, he cannot see her magic – he only sees her face."

"But how can she be fulfilled when the unknowable has no end?"

~ "That which fuels her search is her divine discontent. The masculine seeks adventure, which can be found in the known. But in the being of the woman greater mysteries lie unshown. It is behind the appearances where the man and woman meet, where the horizons of the unknown ever more retreats."

"What then Master, between the unknown and the unknowable differentiates?"

~ "The unknowable is the unexpressed potential, the unknown through the known articulates. The unknown uses components that have been accessed somewhere before, the unknowable elements have never been on the cosmic platform."

"How can the masculine ever these mysteries know when only the feminine into the unknowable goes?"

~ "Within him lies the feminine, which he can develop and cultivate. When in partnership with a woman, proper communication he must create. Approach her as the mystery, in humility it must be done. The interpreter of her unknown dance the masculine must become. From the unknowable she receives her guidance, though what it is she does not know. He must find behind the appearances the meaning she unknowingly shows. Enter now the feminine, like a holy temple she should be seen. With reverence approach her and you'll go where you've never been."

7. The Power of Perspective

"Master, how must life be seen as a burden to endure? Or should imperfection be ignored through focusing on what is pure?"

~ "Life is what your perspective decrees. Either you are in bondage or you are free."

"But what then is the purpose of life?"

~ "Is there a purpose for the butterfly that through the garden flies? It is the flower's artistry that him inspires."

"Is life no more than the unfolding artistry that leads us deeper into a never-ending mystery?" came a voice not before heard as all listened to an artist's words.

~ "It is a perspective chosen by some, but to view life as such benefits everyone."

"If life can be changed by how we perceive, tell me then Master, if you please: Should the wisdom of age or the fountain of youth be that which we choose as our highest truth?"

~ "Choose neither the age or youth of which you speak. It is self-regeneration which you seek. In timeless existence no age exists. It comes in an instant when you cease to resist."

"Do I shape my own destiny or just surrender in trust?"

~ "To surrender to life's unfoldment, that you must. But to refuse to contribute is to not fully live. The quality of the journey is the gift you give to steer your own life and not have it done by the expectations of many and the control of some."

"Is this the case for everyone? Do our chosen perspectives determine the outcome?"

~ "Yes it is so, and the inspiration of your heart. Your unique perspective is the gift you impart. As the Infinite's Intent through your inner senses finds a voice, how you respond is your individual choice."

"In the early dawn, in the first rays of the morn, I must make my way to the work of the day," the crowd did hear a laborer say. Furrowed with care and his clothes well worn. His hands were rough and his coat was torn. "What perspective will help make my burdens light? My body is weary from the toil and strife."

~ With compassion did the master behold that from his burdens the man was old. With a solemn voice the Master spoke: "There is a perspective to ease this yoke. To the glory of all you must your work devote. The greater the burden, the more pressing the need that excellence in the workplace becomes your creed. Acts of devotion that bless everyone, to the Infinite a prayer your work must become."

The labor humbly bowed his head for he heard the wisdom in the words that were said. "Master, truly perspective is the key to ease man's burdens and set him free."

~ "Then mend your clothes and lift up your head. 'Tis not a workplace, but a hallowed temple in which you tread."

As all pondered the words that were said, the Master turned and in a flash he left.

The Runes of the Field of White Magic

The Runes of the Field of Perception of White Magic

The Runes of the Mother Libraries

From the 16th Plate of the Book of Elephant Wisdom

Ech kiye usba nung spaha vilspa krug
Nin hirit spa uk klut za-bong virska
Bilt hufkla spirita ha
Uf balak
Hutl stava nun pa kla usta birk stava

The Mother shall make what was many as one
In the day of no space, this shall be done
The Rose and the Dove, Serpent and the Horse as well
The Eagle and Elephant and Spider, their secrets will tell

Ancient symbols the Mother gave
Shall be hidden in the Elephant's secret cave
Until the day all these libraries shall come
Into the Holy City to be as the Mother's Libraries as one

The 96 Runes of the Mother Libraries

1.

Perpetual Flourishing

2.

Turning Tyrants into Tools

3.

Emphasized Individuality

4.

Majestic Co-creation

5.

The Sacred Language of Inspiration

6.

The Guidance of the Inner Senses

7.

Sustained Vision

8.

Diversity Within

9.

Truth Revealed

10.

Inclusiveness

11.

Impeccability

12.

Expansion of Awareness

13.

Compassionate Understanding

14.

Visionary Experience

15.

Free Flowing Love

16.

Purity of Mind and Heart

17.

Eternal Perfection

18.

Enfolding Embrace

19.

Unfolding Revelation

20.

Celebrating Achievement

21.

The Power of Symbols

22.

Effortless Mastery

23.

Majestic Moments

24.

Birthing Magic

25.

Achieving Potential

26.

Endless Growth

27.

Becoming Purified

28.

Expansive Vision

29.

Omnipresent Grace

30.

Perfect Grace

31.

Wisdom in Action

32.

Delicate Artistry

33.

Life-giving Presence

34.

Purposeful Support

35.

Trusted Intuition

36.

Interconnectedness Respected

37.

Bridge of Light and Love

38.

Building Confidence

39.

Flowing with the River of Life

40.

Mystery Revealed

41.

Vibrant Living

42.

The Impetus of Passion

43.

Self-determined Quality of the Journey

44.

Purposeful Living

45.

Healing Sigils

46.

Wings of Hope

47.

Power in Action

48.

Infinite Precision

49.

Master Weaver

50.

Patience Unfolding

51.

Releasing Old Patterns

52.

Soaring Flight

53.

Releasing Programs

54.

Ascension Attitudes

55.

Fulfilled Expectations

56.

Field of Light

57.

Reunion of Love and Light

58.

Universal Language

59.

Family of Gods and Angels

60.

Mature Spirituality

61.

Humble Search for Perception

62.

Sacred Spark of Perfection

63.

Magical Incantations

64.

Strong Trust

65.

Unshakeable Faith

66.

Adventure of Discovery

67.

Respect for Life

68.

Joyous Dance of Life

69.

Expression of Individuality

70.

Regenerated Physicality

71.

Power of Unity

72.

Sacred Alchemy

73.

**Strength through
Self-discipline**

74.

Creativity Unveiled

75.

Magic Materialized

76.

From Intention to Form

77.

Deep Wisdom

78.

Impeccable Intention

79.

Cooperative Endeavors

80.

Lightness of Being

81.

The Sword of Discernment

82.

Unerring Surrender

83.

Infallibility through Integrity

84.

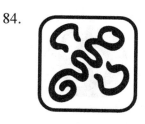

Transformation through Magic

85.

Herald of the Dawn

86.

Empowering Wayshower

87.

Beckoning Mystery

88.

Instinctual Wisdom

89.

Sacred Fire

90.

Primal Building Blocks

91.

Courageous Trailblazer

92.

Steward of Sacred Knowledge

93.

Sacredness of Matter

94.

Evolution of Magical Abilities

95.

Treasure of Ancient Knowledge

96.

Release of Limitations

The Seven Steps of Mastery

Step 3

Acknowledging Oneness

To right a wrong judges and divides. To acknowledge wholeness uplifts and heals.

Almine

The Field of Perception of Healing

The Wheel for the Runes of the Field of Perception of Healing

Sersavich Nestavu Heraset

Wholeness through Remembered Oneness

The Seven Perceptions of Healing remind us that behind the seeming separate expressions of individuated life, the unified field of the heart joins all in oneness.

The Restoration of the True Nature of Mastery by Cutting the Ties that Bind

The Wheel of Perpetual Regeneration Through Trusting
Self-sovereignty

Illness and injury result from imagined cords of limitation.
In releasing these, and in the memory of our indestructible oneness,
are we healed.

Almine

The Gas Discharge Visualization Assessment for Determining the Effectiveness of Healing Methods

A study was initiated in the presence of the healer Almine to ascertain visible and scientific measures of changes on the biological systems of a small group of subjects. The Gas Discharge Visualization (GDV) Bioelectrography camera was used. The images show before and after views of the subjects following a 12-minute healing session with Almine. Each subject demonstrated holes, cords, and weakened areas in their energy fields prior to the healing, with removal of cord and holes and overall strengthening of fields following the healing session.

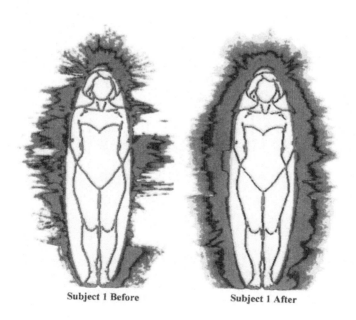

Subject 1 Before   Subject 1 After

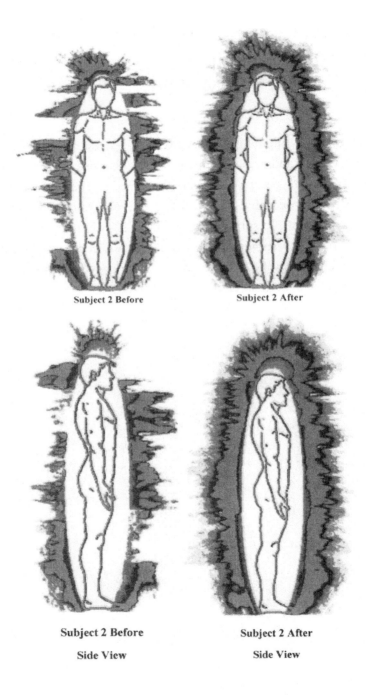

Subject 2 Before

Subject 2 After

Subject 2 Before

Side View

Subject 2 After

Side View

136

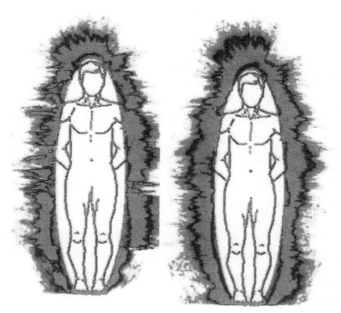

Subject 3 Before   **Subject 3 After**

Eighteen Incorrect Assumptions
Cutting the Ties that Bind

1. We have the incorrect assumption that the elements are an
    absolutely essential part of individuation: that earth, fire, air and
    water comprise physical life and light, frequency, energy, and life
    force comprise the intangible areas of existence.

    Note: the primal non-atomic element is indivisible, matterless
    matter that forms and unforms without clustering.

2. We believe the human boundaries to apply to everyone, even
    though the ancient gods have come among men, walking in
    forgetfulness. Human limitations are made by the belief systems
    of the ages and the teachings of the supposed unalterable natural
    laws.

3. The belief in the transient nature of physical life and the
    permanent nature of the soul and spirit dissolves when we realize
    that we have been in a triangular mirrored reality, alternating
    our attention between them. The body, soul and spirit are just
    the vehicles of our expression as we 'travel' through these linear
    stages of change from one mirror to another.

4. The incorrect assumption that opposites are separate and that
    they need to be hostile to one another must be corrected by
    first realizing that they can be mutually inspiring rather than in
    conflict. Their apparent separation is due to the placement of our
    awareness on one pole to the exclusion of the other.

5. The inevitable nature of karma is created by our choice of
    learning through repetition, rather than self-examination and the

perceptions yielded by remaining both the observer of our actions and the observed. The punitive nature of life is a fallacy.

6. Decay and aging, assumed to be a natural and inevitable state of existence, are the result of the depletion of energy in polarity (called inertia). This is not the case however, the minute we move into a different reality such as dynamic oneness. The choice is ours.

7. Some of the biggest perceived captors of awareness are space and time. They are however not the tyrants our beliefs have made them, but rather fluid tools for us to wield. The tool of time is a common reference point for interaction among people, but an individual can slow or speed it up.

8. There is a common assumption that the body is less conscious and therefore less holy than the soul or spirit. All three are the vehicles of experience in the three stages of life inside the mirrored life of opposites. The true self is seasonless in its eternal observation of the play.

9. The 'negative' emotions of anger, pain, guilt, fear and protectiveness must not be allowed to contaminate a spiritual life. This incorrect premise does not take into consideration the positive use of these emotions as indicators of areas we have not yet embraced in oneness and taken responsibility for.

10. Because of the adversarial affect of living in a reality where life around us is a reflection, we assume that adversity is an unavoidable state of existence. By overcoming the tendency to value one pole more than another, life becomes a cooperative venture.

11. Life as an expression comes from releasing judgment and taking
responsibility for outer manifestations. But the incorrect premise
that opposites exist as separate entities is still present. Within
the problem, the solution is already present. Within the answer,
another question lies. Opposites are indivisibly one, appearing as
opposites only because of emphases of perspective.

12. The illusion that flaws or mistakes exist within the unfoldment
of the perfection of the universe is born of limited perspectives.
Heinous deeds that shock our innocence come about only from
our resistance to graceful change. Through the surrendered life we
know there is nothing to fix.

13. The inevitability of infirmities and illnesses reveals itself to
be optional after all, when we realize that all unwholeness is
created by the separativeness of mind. All illness is therefore
psychosomatic.

14. The concept of childbearing as the successful fulfillment of
everyone's destiny is the flawed perspective of a limited life of
mortality. An immortal society steps off the concept of life and
death cycles. If death ends as part of the evolved state of being
that we are reaching for, so does birth.

15. The dependency on others is seen as a necessity. This in part
arises from the premise that birth and childhood are inevitabilities
and that the young must be cared for. In a deathless society one's
being becomes their sustenance. Though obscured by duality, this
truth has always been a reality.

16. The law of compensation has been accepted for eons as a valid
assumption because of seeing ourselves as separate from the
rest of life. More of one has always been less of another. This is

dependent on our perspective however, since including the world within our consciousness (becoming one with all things) allows any part of existence to flourish without owing. It is the self, giving to the self.

17. The pervasive nature of tribalism, the desire to seek uniform elements in others, stems from man's need to affirm himself by finding mirrors that reflect similarities. The flaw in this perception is that all we see is ourself, for nothing other than what we are expressing can ever be seen.

18. It is often believed that there is a dysfunctional relationship possible with the personality of Source, whom we can bargain with and pacify in order to prevent punishment and otherwise expect favors from. This personality is given certain attributes such as mercy, vengeance, and other incongruous and flawed qualities. The origin of these projections stem from our less than perfect relationships with our parents, as well as our unwillingness to acknowledge our vital role in creating our life's circumstances. Our greatest contribution to forming our realities comes from our chosen perspectives and consequent attitudes. We are the co-creators to the quality of our journey.

The Seven Perceptions of Healing

1. War and Peace

When the sun's first rays announced the break of day, people waited to hear what the Master would say. Rumors of wars in distant lands and raging battles between the sons of man had disquieted the peoples' hearts. They wondered what wisdom the Master would impart.

~ "The battles of war in your hearts begin when war and peace both rage within. Whenever more value on one pole is bestowed, the fight to survive that which is denied makes it so."

"Silence your fears for against you they strive, failure they bring when instead you would thrive. A light you are that irradiates the world. In humility let wings of majesty unfurl. If with devotion for mastery you strive, you cannot believe that you can be victimized. Only shadows that within you hide can cause inconvenience that in your life you'll find. In silent trust choose realities that inspire, support them with your faith until they produce the quality you desire."

"What is faith Master?" a priest's voice inquired.

~ "The strong vision you hold of that which you desire. Not with the need of the heart or the intent to control but with glad expectations of what will unfold. Through your inspired vision steer the course, then let it be fulfilled through the Intent of Source. Then shall the war of the ego be stilled as it pits itself no more against the Infinite's Will."

A philosopher stood forth and spoke his mind: "Master, what is the destiny of humankind? Tell us please of the war between the conditioned and natural man, if peace should be found, is it possible that it can?"

~ "Pristine is the pattern of evolving man. While yet a child this is cluttered by the social learning received from his parents' hands. He identifies by deeds that are done. How others see him is how he becomes. Until through coping with life, personalities form and an unnatural perception of himself is formed.

"Stifled like diamonds lying in the dust, the natural man hides but emerge he must. In the battle to express, his freedom to gain, the natural man fights on driven by pain. How should there be peace you say. How can the natural expression of pristine man take place?"

"Nothing wields to a greater light unless its value is first seen, unless it is given its rights."

"But Master, what possible purpose can the artificial serve? What acknowledgment could it from us deserve?"

~ "Like the grains of sand that oppose the sprouting seed develop the strength that the emerging plant needs, so too the obstacles of the artificial retard growth's speed. In the laws of mechanics, this more power provides, which helps individuation's unique contribution survive. When a layer of artificiality clears at times, speed returns and life can thrive. Thus the natural and artificial work together like the wings of a butterfly.

2. Sacred Sexuality

A young man asked, "Master, when is sexuality sacred, a tool to bring forth the divine?" The crowd was silent for none had thought of sexuality as sublime.

~ "A question that has many answers you will find: It is not only a tool to perpetuate humankind. Wisdom it is to know that for so much more it was designed."

143

"In humility you must enter the temple of sexuality, that it may set you free from bondage through its unleashed potency."

"But Master, like a wildfire it rages and its power frightens me. My discipline it could shatter and damage my spirituality. Through ages churches told us to approach it cautiously. How then could it deliver the ultimate liberty?"

"Those who wished to control and man's mind dominate have said its only purpose is to procreate. No one ever told you its power opens Heaven's Gate."

"What is this gate you speak of Master? Where can it be found?"

An excited whisper rippled through the crowd as they wondered if the Master this great secret would tell.

~ "If you want to know it, in oneness you must dwell. For only there does it appear: resurrection's gate. Like a gem that in the high heart you can locate. A forgotten chakra that in duality no one knows, in oneness like a turquoise gem brightly does it glow. Seven in duality, but eight chakras in oneness show."

"Through the ecstasy of your union, in deep love and bliss is the gate thrust open, a new reality revealed by this. To dwell beyond the opposition of the building blocks of life, for it is in their heart where the root of duality lies."

"Master, what is so exceptional about the turquoise chakra's role? Is it just through union with another that its function will unfold?"

~ "It is the seat of magic, where inner and outer spaces meet. The doorway to the primordial matter that from duality sets you free. To the one who lives in celibacy there is another way: To become at one with nature in his inner and outer states."

"But in entering through the gateway, will we not fade away? Will we not leave our loved ones who behind us must stay?"

~ "On the Earthly plane you stay, though reality is lived another way. Your body will appear as other's do, though life will have altered for you. Fluidly life will respond to the inspired intent of your heart. As co-creator with the Infinite, you will play your part."

"Your partner is a sacred opportunity to see beyond duality. Approach them with humility. Your partner is a gateway to eternity. Let not the sun set on the awareness' song unsung. "

"Let not the discovery of your partner's mystery be a deed undone. See beyond appearances that the veil may melt away. Every layer thus revealed exposes a miracle each day."

"The techniques in monasteries taught of practices that through sex, consciousness can increase...what then Master, do you say of these?"

~ "They increase the man's awareness but the woman does not gain. To enhance oneself at the cost of another ultimately brings pain. The increase that they offer is still within duality. To approach your partner without technique, but rather as a mystery, with the passion of eternal love, touches the face of eternity."

3. Self-love

"Master, where does the love for my neighbor come from? When I cannot create what I do not feel?"

~ "The source of love for others I shall reveal. It begins with self-love, like much else does too. All aspects of self-love begin with you. You cannot love another before you love yourself too."

"How then do I love the self? Is it through awareness or something else"

~ "If loving your neighbor requires that the miracle of their life be seen, you must see them as they are, not as they have been. In examining the self, leave the past behind. It is what you express today that you must find. Self-knowledge ever unfolds, that is true. But it is a requisite for self-love in you."

"Be kind and patient with yourself at all times. This will create tolerance with humankind. Blind spots in perception are present in everyone you meet. Thus in yourself they must also be. All that exists serves a purpose we cannot see. If it did not, it would not continue to be. "

"What purpose could be served by the flaws of all?"

~ "They shape individual perspectives, nothing more."

"Why could they not have been gone before?"

~ "A timing device, they create our strengths to thrive. Just like the chicken must fight to have the strength to survive. When they release, through the winds of perception blown away, energy is bestowed, for storage units of resources are they."

"Thus the folly of man holds great resources. Master, is that what you say?"

~ "Yes. View this day your own mistakes and those of others this way. That self-acceptance and forgiveness take place."

"Who is it that determines what blind spots must stay and which ones will release, by perception done away?"

~ "The unfolding cosmos moves in majestic beauty on its way - a work of art in progress in which we may participate. It is the Creator's design that determines what shadows must stay. The blindness of your neighbor has an artistic role to play."

"Honor the perfection of Creation even though we cannot see the full perfection of the artistry the Creator forms so masterfully."

"If I cannot see the full artistic glory, how can I understand the contribution of his folly?"

~ "Because the pattern of the whole hides in all its parts. Do not search for it with your eyes, feel it with your heart. Behind the appearances it slumbers, the message of eternity: All of life is innocent, we dwell in purity."

"How must I see the innocence of one who strikes a blow?"

~ "It is in the sacrifice he makes in order the lessons to bestow. That there is something pillaged in your life, he comes to show. Once you get the lesson then his flaw will go. At times he is your guidance, blocking your way ahead so that you may choose a different path instead. He also comes to strengthen certain qualities within by showing you what you are not, that greater understanding of yourself may begin."

"Know yourself to be an expression of the Infinite, unfolding endlessly. Know that this neighbor is too, an endless mystery. Let reverent love for all be found, for within the darkest shadow, light abounds. Respect yourself, for wherever you are is holy ground."

4. Freedom of Choice

"Where is there freedom of choice? Where is life dictated by fate?"

~ "To be fully free to choose, master time and space. They are the dual ties that bind. To master them, freedom of choice you'll find."

"What choices are gained, what is already fore-ordained? How does the individual choose, but still Infinite Will obey?"

~ The Master paused as though to contemplate. "Think of time as lines of movement through space. A map there is of how time flows, a pattern of choice for those who know. The pattern of fluid lines represents the guidelines created by Infinite Intent."

"Master, are these lines ever rearranged? Are they permanent or are they changed?"

~ "In the new year of the Chinese, the map changes its lines. Through the eyes of the Infinite but a moment has gone by."

"How Master, can freedom upon these pathways be maintained? How can we change the course of life? Please explain."

~ "By rotating your map through a perspective change. The lines of time intersect. Multiple choices does this represent. The options you choose are still part of the map of Infinite Intent."

Yet again the Master paused, finding the best way to explain: "Not only can directions of your life be changed, but the rotation of the map itself can be attained. Realities by our attitudes are maintained. By shifting our perspectives, the attitudes too are changed. Life around us can be greatly rearranged."

"Do I understand then Master, what it is you say: not only can directions by our choices change, but our reality as a whole can remade? This is done by seeing life in a different way?"

~ "It is correct what you say." The Master, foreseeing a question yet to come answered: "This is possible for everyone."

"What can we do to master the choices that await, and what of those who are ignorant of the differences they can make?"

~ "Fear of change blocks possibilities for many on their way. They seek predictability and thus travel the same road over and over again. Through sensitive awareness shall you find options open to you. Through the inspiration of your heart shall you know what you must do. Know that failure does not exist and boldly you must go. Through eternity do you travel upon the pathways of time, either in loops of caution, or on unexplored time lines."

"A scholar spoke in measured tones: "Master, the answer to a question I must know: What are days out of time that on other calendars one can find? Can one travel backwards to pasts left behind?"

The crowd in silence pondered what they had heard. Only a few could comprehend the learned scholar's words.

~ "Profound indeed the meaning of a day out of time. On a time map it is where many lines entwine. Converging on a single spot, many possibilities are combined."

After a pause the scholar spoke, a question in his voice: "But a day out of time implies more than just the increase of choice. It seems to say that from the map of time we can be free, as though a portal it is to another reality?"

~ "There are seven time maps available, each expressing Infinite Intent perfectly. Seven dimensions through seven perspectives do they represent, each a unique reality. Through living their perspectives on that day, they can become part of your life permanently."

"As a master then, can you choose the many options thus revealed: To walk again at a time once lived, that the past may be healed. Or boldly forge a new pathway by treading the unknown, thus for others new horizons by example may be shown. When you walk the lines of time, open to other dimensions too, greater awakenings will occur bringing a life of miracles to you."

5. Understanding Evil

"Master, what is evil and what is good?"

~ "In three aspects evil is misunderstood. That which has been named thus are three entirely different things. This is what such confusion brings."

"Of these named, what is the greatest evil that plagues humankind?"

~ "The greatest is unnamed, in garments of good it hides behind. The greatest evil is the social conditioning of mind. The evil that is named of its own accord does not arise. The destructuring of light it is, that is of old programs combined. The more you cling to that which is known, the more destructuring has to claim its own."

"Destructuring has value. Why do we reject its cause?"

The crowd grew still as the Master paused, "From fear comes the desire to keep what is known. Destructuring is shunned because it brings the unknown."

"What other sources of evil, or shadow, can we find?"

~ "There is the real shadow of your light, created by your judgment of what is wrong and what is right. False shadows made from the beliefs of man flood reality, value judgments of duality. Distorted views by religions bestowed seek the minds of man to hold. False light and false shadow, yesterday's belief systems bestow. "

"How can we resolve the matter of evil in our lives, that change may from fluid surrender be derived?"

~ "Do not let the shadows of your life be your guide. Rather steer your course by that which does inspire. By holding on to events of hardship from the past, you let them define the present and make the memories last. When loss has been suffered, something else had room to grow. Find the gifts of hardship, then let the memories go."

"How does one release memories when the pain sears our souls? Tell us Master please, that we may know."

~ "As you travel through your days, know that life is not what it seems. The cycles you have travelled are but vanishing dreams."

"Why is it Master, that we value shadows so? That in our imagination, larger than life it grows?"

~ "Consider now the reality in which all humans dwell, and the reason for overvaluing I now shall tell: The quest of every being is to know himself well. But surrounded by mirrors of belief systems, who he is he cannot tell. There he sees what he is not, thus from his shadow, knowledge of himself he got."

"Is there another misperception – a third? Clearer ways to look at evil we have not heard?"

~ "The desire to save and bring into the light, makes shadows linger beyond the night. Like a discordant tone a musician plays, our misplaced intentions make shadows stay."

"To right a wrong still judges and divides. To acknowledge wholeness, uplifts and inspires. Know then that anything that in the moment exists serves a purpose, though unrecognized it is. Find the purpose it comes to fulfill and instead of fear, a shadow wisdom will instill."

The Gift of Deep Sleep

*In sleep do we encounter the realms of inner space. In mastery do we
walk in rest and sleep in wakefulness...*

Almine

Statistics indicate that sleep deprivation is on the rise. Once the
natural and regenerative gift of man, it is now becoming a rare and
prized commodity.

Lack of sleep impacts the consciousness of man in several ways.
The one trapped in the mirrors of the egoic self uses the four stages of
dreaming to guide his life and to facilitate graceful rather than traumatic
change. Guidance is obtained by interpreting the dream symbols[2] that
speak through dreams, as a language from the psyche.

For the master, who has left the world of mirrors and lives from
his pristine state of being beyond contracted or expanded awareness,
there are seven levels of dreaming available. Each offers guidance by
revealing levels of potential that are accessible for articulation. The
contribution of the deeper levels of the psyche enriches the experience
of every day life. Shallow or disrupted sleep on the other hand, produces
superficial and shallow living. Shallowness of living increases the
tendency towards a materialistic society.

Causes of Insomnia and Shallow Sleep States

Since the problem of sleep deprivation has become global, the causes
themselves must therefore also be occurring globally. We are bombarded
by hostile waveforms from cell phones, cell towers and many other
sources. This causes geopathic stress and tension in the body.

---

[2] A free digital copy of Almine's Dream Dictionary, 2nd Edition is available here: http://
alminewisdom.com/products/dream-dictionary.

As populations increase, so too does noise, until it becomes harder and harder to find silence. The noise pollution of the planet comes in the form of frequency discernable to the ear as well as the 'black' indiscernible noise of the radio waves bombarding us each second. Noise pulls us out of the moment where sleep is found, and further impedes our ability to fall asleep by creating an inner dialogue of the mind.

Pollution, chemical additives to our food and hostile substances absorbed through the skin from toiletries etc., as well as other challenges to the immune system, cause allergies. They may not register as a familiar allergic reaction, but the adrenal response may cause a more rapid heartbeat and tension in the body. This physiological state of emergency prevents the relaxed state that precipitates sound sleep.

The use of birth control pills, antibiotics (also present in some meat products) and steroids have been promoted by the pharmaceutical industry, without the necessary education on their safe use and the avoidance of negative effects. The indiscriminate use of these substances has caused a pandemic of candidiasis[3] – the overgrowth of fungus in the body. The fungus initially disrupts the proper function of the digestive track, preventing the absorption of nutrients and eventually affects the entire body. The amino acid, tryptophan, is vital for deep sleep, as are the B vitamins and some minerals. Their absence furthermore causes deficiencies in the pineal and pituitary glands, which creates the disturbances of over-active thoughts and inner dialogue.

When the liver is deficient, it stores that which it cannot metabolize in other areas of the body. Its most difficult burden is getting rid of heavy metals from cooking pots and pans, water pipes and other sources. The heavy metal toxicity causes distortion in the personality, producing symptoms such as fear of being alone, fear of the future, mood swings,

---

[3] See *How to Facilitate the Healing of Chronic and Systemic Disease* book for a list of candidiasis symptoms. The list is also available on the *Handbook for Healers* website at http://www.handbookforhealers.com/candida-symptoms/.

as well as disturbed dreams. The colors green and blue strengthen the organs of the immune and nervous systems, but the green found in nature is largely absent from our cities. The full spectrum of blue light from the sky also cannot reach the eyes because of pollution of the air, tinted contact lenses, glasses, sunglasses and windows, thus depriving us of this light therapy.

The dialogue within the mind is used by an individual to repress unprocessed, negative emotions. The more we repress, the more complexity arises in our life.

Solutions and Tools for Deep Sleep through Inner Harmony and Balance

In order to find a solution for such a diversity of causes, one must search for common elements within the solution for each situation. One such common element is frequency, and another is breath. The absorption of proper nutrients through establishing and maintaining a healthy gastrointestinal tract is a third approach that forms a component of nearly all solutions applicable to sound and uninterrupted sleep.

Breath

Suppressed trauma is held in the gap between the breaths. It manifests as rigidity in the diaphragm that impedes the proper movement of the lungs. Birth and rebirth trauma also tightens the psoas muscle.

Tools

1. *The Sacred Breaths of Arasatma*: available at http:// spiritualjourneys.com and Amazon.com.

2. *Aranash Suba Yoga* for the release of the trauma of birth and rebirth held in the psoas muscle. Available at http:// spiritualjourneys.com.

Nutrients

1. The comprehensive 2-hour audio lecture, *How to Facilitate the Healing of Chronic and Systemic Disease[4]*, which accompanies the book of the same name, has been developed to eliminate heavy metals, candidiasis and chemicals from the body.

2. The spiritual reason for deficient digestion, absorption and elimination is the inability to 'stomach' occurrences in your environment. Perception is a potent way to help lift us up and over negative emotions that resist our ability to 'absorb' or accept life.

Nine Steps to Recapitulate Life

An excerpt from *Journey to the Heart of God.*

This process provides the necessary perception to help with the release of resistance to life:

In recapitulation, we go through the events that still 'pull our strings' to find the lesson, the contract and to identify our role. We take a careful look at what the mirrors show: Is it something we are, or something we have yet to develop? Is it something we judge, or something we have given away? What is the gift? We see through past life regressions[5] what part of the bigger puzzle we are trying to solve. As we recapitulate more and more of our life, one day we find we have achieved a miracle: the inner dialog of the mind has made way for silence, and within the silence, all things are possible.

Any person or situation that still brings up disturbing emotions or a knee-jerk reaction should be carefully examined. Trace it back to the first occurrence where a similar event caused a similar response. Then extract from the experience the core insights by asking nine questions.

---

[4] See http://alminewisdom.com/collections/belvaspata/products/bvp-chronic-disease-audio.
[5] See *Life of Miracles* for more information on past life regression.

Note: The first five questions assist us in seeing what is really going on. Use the intellect for this part because it was designed to help us discern what is behind surface appearances.

1. What is the lesson? Look for the lesson that our higher self wishes us to embrace. For example, the lesson may be that we need to speak our truth. It could manifest as laryngitis, or someone may appear to mirror to us that we frequently suppress our voice. He or she may violate our boundaries to get our attention. We need to protect ourselves by voicing our truth that this behavior is unacceptable. Accepting the unacceptable isn't saintly, it is dysfunctional.

2. What is the contract? Everyone who interacts with us has made an agreement prior to this incarnation to assist with our growth and for us to assist in theirs. They may have agreed to push us over the edge, and we may do likewise for them. Ask, "What is the contract we are playing out?" It is with great love that many agreed while in the spirit world to be our catalysts. When we are in perfect equilibrium, there is no growth so it is a signal to the universe to knock us off balance so the lessons may continue. Thus we pull relationships into our lives that test us in every way imaginable.

3. What is the role? Am I playing the victim? Am I playing the teacher or the student? What role am I playing within this contract? Also look at the role the other person is playing. For example, we may have a tyrant in our life. It may be our spouse, mother or boss. Once you establish that, see who you are in relation to that person's role. Remember, we may change our role at any time because we create our reality.

4. What is the mirror? We pull relationships into our life that mirror one of the following things: an aspect of who we are, what we have given away, what we still place judgment on, or what we haven't developed yet. For example, if our innocence is gone, we may find ourselves intensely attracted to a young person. If we have given our integrity away, we might fall in love with a missionary who, in our eyes, represents integrity. Another thing that can be mirrored is that which we judge. If we have problems dealing with people who lie, then we are judging them and therefore attract liars.

5. What is the gift? Every person we encounter has come to give us a gift and to receive one as well. This applies even with the most casual acquaintance. Ask, "What gift am I supposed to give this person?" It may be something as simple as offering him the gift of unconditional love; or we may recognize something beautiful in him that nobody else has seen. We may genuinely listen to someone and for the first time in years, they feel heard and understood.

Note: The last four questions deal with our attitudes surrounding the answers to the first five questions.

6. Can I allow? This is the point of discerning what has to be allowed, what has to be changed, and finding the courage to act. Imagine yourself as the water in a river. If a rock is in front of you, should you oppose it or flow around the rock? We have masterfully created every situation in our life, even the rock. Is this a test of flexibility and surrender? Or is this a battle for us to fight? A battle is only worth fighting if the stakes are worth winning. If you have already learned the lesson, no need to re-fight this battle.

7. Can I accept? We cannot accept the painful things that happen to us unless we begin to see the perfection underlying the web of appearances. A common belief is that we were placed on the wheel of reincarnation, suffering lifetime after lifetime, until we have lived enough lives to become perfect. We have been created perfectly, with the ability to be a creator. Thoughts combined with emotions create our environment. The heart is like a microphone: the stronger the emotions, the stronger the universe's response to manifest our desires. But the universe doesn't discriminate; it will manifest whatever we think – positive or negative. It is important that we accept that we have co-created the situation, which removes any feelings of having things done 'to' us.

8. Can I release? To release is to let go of the energy surrounding the person or event. If we don't release, we keep it alive by feeding it energy through thoughts (sometimes subconsciously). Even if someone has violated us in some way, working through these steps to gain the larger insights behind the appearances, changes the focus to an eternal perspective. It reveals the perfection underlying the appearances.

9. Can I be grateful? If we have gone through the previous eight steps and can feel true gratitude for the insights gained, it raises consciousness. Gratitude is a powerful attitude that can assist us to transfigure into a higher state of being. It changes stumbling blocks into steppingstones.

If we have completed the first eight steps and don't feel gratitude, going through them again to gain even deeper insights will help.

It is time for a more comprehensive understanding by the light promoters of what we deem our 'undesirable' pieces, or emotions. Too many believe they fulfill their part by focusing only on light and love.

But over-polarizing towards the light is as detrimental to the evolution of awareness as over-polarizing towards the dark. In both instances stagnation occurs and evolution of awareness is retarded.

It is part of the universal law of compensation that we strengthen that which we oppose. This applies not only to traits within ourselves, but similarly to traits in others. On the other hand, acknowledging the perfection underlying the appearances surrounding irritation lessens its hold on us and provides increased perception. Through perception comes transfiguration until eventually rage reveals those parts of life worth keeping. The rage that does remain becomes a valuable tool to extract insights from experience.

Frequency

Frequency is the sculptor of individuated life. It hones and chisels the experiences that manifest in our life. It is key to mental, emotional and physical wellness, and is the bringer of dynamic balance to our experiences and responses upon our eternal journey.

We express it overtly as the emotions we feel, and more subtly as the song of the self; the frequency we emit as the signature of who we are in any given moment. The frequency is like a never-ending river that changes every moment. It can be changed and guided by us to enhance its beneficial influence in all areas of our lives, including deep and peaceful sleep.

Frequency is a powerful ally in our quest for sleep in the following ways:

1. In the hands of a master who has studied frequency as the movement of awareness through space, it can combat hostile waveforms, and the deliberate interference of invading frequencies from others. In this function, it is the most powerful tool available to reclaim our restful, sacred space.

The music produced for this form of sound healing contains not only the 'white' sound that is audible to the ear, but also 'black' sound that is carried within the notes. This combats noise pollution that is audible and inaudible – referred to as 'black noise'.[6] By combining what is known to mystics as white light frequencies with black light frequencies, that which is illusion-based such as lack, aging and disease, subliminal programming, HAARP, nanotechnology, vaccines and more are neutralized.

2. The sound of the voice of an individual should be like his or her own sound healing device. This takes place only when the individual lives a self-examined life that increases its perception and consciousness each day. Perception yields pure emotions and pure emotions yield increased perception. This mutually inspirational relationship between perception (light) and emotion (frequency) eliminates the inner war that causes bodily inflammation and dialogue of the mind, keeping us from peaceful sleep.

3. Sound healing for health or sleep provides the missing frequencies for one who has forgotten the oneness of all life. The one who has awakened from the mirrored world of duality, can remind others of this elevated state by providing those frequencies within their voice.

Closing

Sleeplessness has come from the disruption of frequencies by many invading factors. The key to reversing this globally rising trend is to restore the frequencies to their pristine state by taking time for deep, meaningful living, eating healthy foods, and sound healing. What we have created, we can also uncreate: the restoration of the peace of the future lies in our hands.

---

[6] See sound healing products at http://angelsoundhealing.com.

The Runes of the
Field of Healing

The Runes of the Field of Perception of Healing

The Runes of the Sacred Order of the Butterfly

Kaa ying pang ho. Baa ling eeya hu nan
Pee tee ee ha yut. Bee eenem sta
Oyo kaa hem. Aayaa paaye eeho
Kaa veenyam spaa ooya bana veem

Ancient the tale of these sacred runes
Mother to Her children gave the butterfly runes
The long ancient libraries that guarded them well
The story of the butterfly runes do tell
The holy Mother made them Her children to delight
She filled them with Her love and Her light
She wove them into a magical robe
That Her Love they would feel no matter where She roamed

A Fall did come and separated they were
The runes were hidden by Her
Preserved in a land that in the East does lie
They will come forth when there is no more time

The 96 Runes of the Order
of the Sacred Butterfly

1.

Loving Creativity
This rune is drawn when it's time
to let go of the old and allow the
new to appear. It is also a time
of assessment so that lessons
and insights might be brought
forward.

2.

Purity in Action
Mind can be obscured by social
conditioning, personal labels of
identity, or unresolved issues
clouding it with emotion. If
any of these are present, they
must be cleared to produce true
perception.

3.

Impeccability of Being
This rune is a warning that
action can no longer be delayed
or damage of some sort will be
incurred. View the landscape
of your life to see which areas
produce tension and analyze what
action is required.

4.

Majesty in Manifestation
Don't allow others or events
to pull you out of your core
strength and balance. There is a
moment to act and a moment not
to – inner calmness will reveal
which moment is before you.

5.

Beauty Revealed
The restoration of white magic is as of yet in its infancy amongst man. This rune indicates that a window of opportunity to perform white magic is before you.

6.

Silence of the Mind
This rune is an indication that an obstacle to the flow of events has been encountered. Remove obstacles without by removing obstacles within. Search for areas where you are not fluidly cooperating with life.

7.

Transfiguration
When enough insights are gained, life must transfigure to the next level. During transfiguration the old coping mechanisms will no longer serve and should be relinquished with grace. Expect life to be different.

8.

Harmony
When this rune is drawn in a situation, harmony will result from the interaction. This indicates that the energy of all involved are in harmony.

9.

Learning Opportunities
This rune indicates that a
journey of discovery has begun.
The learning will be a pleasant
adventure unless the rune is
upside down, in which case it
signifies that learning comes
through opposition.

10.

Climax of Experience
The journey you have been on
is about to peak. If you've been
suffering, it's about to get a
little worse before improving. If
you've been prospering, expect
it to peak before dropping lower.
If upside down, more energy is
needed to bring the journey to
culmination.

11.

Alignment.
When we align ourselves with
the will of the Infinite through
listening to the guidance of
our heart, great power is at our
disposal. Be still that you might
be guided to act in the right way
at the right time.

12.

Door of Opportunity
This rune has no upside down
position and always indicates
there is a door in front of you
to knock on. Some effort from
your side is required to make the
opportunity happen.

13.

14.

Service

There is an opportunity to make a great difference in someone's life. True service can be rendered by empowering another.

Autonomy

This rune is drawn when outer circumstances must be changed by changing within. Find what piece of yourself it mirrors and give it love and forgiveness. In this way the outer is changed layer by layer.

15.

16.

Pre-emptive Moment

A rare opportunity has presented itself to secure success for a future venture. This rune could be called 'the early bird catches the worm'. When inverted, there is nothing to be done at this moment for future success.

Spiritual Warriorship

Every battle in life is a battle for self- knowledge. If it cannot produce this, do not engage. You strengthen that which you oppose. When upside down, you are fighting the wrong battle.

17.

Acknowledgment
This rune says it is time to acknowledge either your own accomplishments or those of another. Without celebrating success, the journey may become overwhelming.

18.

Harmonious Compatibility
Compatibility and partnership will be present in interactions when this rune is drawn. Smooth interaction is promoted.

19.

Strategy
Careful strategy needs to be devised, sometimes taking one step back in order to take two steps forward. When upside down, your strategy needs to be revised.

20.

Higher Assistance
Energies need to be directed toward a desired outcome by calling on divine assistance. When upside down, it warns you've been too nearsighted in thinking you can do it alone.

21.

Harnessing Resources
There are resources at your disposal that you've overlooked. They are ample to swing your endeavors from failure to success. When inverted, it means there are not enough resources to successfully complete the project. To do so, you must increase the resources or change the requirements.

22.

Unorthodox Innovation
The solution you seek requires methods that are definitely beyond the norm. Act from your highest truth, with careful consideration for the consequences, but discard the opinions of others. A decision completely off the beaten path needs to be considered.

23.

Purging
Something needs to be weeded out of your life. It could be an obsolete coping mechanism or viewpoint of your own, or incompatible players in your environment. When upside down, this change is truly overdue.

24.

Confrontation
It is necessary to speak your heart. Confrontation does not have to be negative, especially when it's spoken with compassion. Upside down, an unpleasant confrontation is coming.

25.

Relationship
Friendship or a partner of destiny is at hand. It could also mean the renewal, through enhanced awareness, of an existing relationship. When this rune is upside down, avoid the relationship.

26.

Sovereignty
Action needs to be taken from your highest identity as a being as vast as the cosmos having a human experience. Do not let yourself be drawn in by appearances.

27.

Heritage
When right side up, you are reminded of the gifts of ancestral or star lineages that are available to you. Inverted, it warns that you are bringing weaknesses of ancestors or star lineages into the moment.

28.

Call to Destiny
In every life, key moments present themselves like doorways. Sometimes great courage is required to step over the edge of a cliff. When destiny calls, follow it. Upside down, it could indicate a lost opportunity.

29.

Unexpected Results
Reason cannot guide you into
the future, only your heart
can. Reason can only predict
based on that which has already
been. What lies ahead will be
unexpected in its outcome. When
upside down, an unpleasant
unexpected outcome awaits.

30.

Healing of the Heart
The circumstances for which you
draw this rune will be healing
to your heart. It will promote
emotional well-being and
affirmation. Upside down, this
could be a hurtful situation.

31.

Interdimensional Assistance
The world is alive with mysteries
and hidden kingdoms wanting to
befriend man. Interdimensional
assistance is being offered.

32.

The Wayshower
Watch for signs in your
environment. Indicators will
clearly provide the answers you
seek. Upside down, indicators
have been missed.

33.

Timing
This advocates restraint and patience. Your heart will tell you when it's the right moment to act. Inverted, actions have been taken that are ill-timed. Perhaps you should regroup.

34.

Undercurrent
Be aware that all is not what it seems. True motives and accompanying emotions are being hidden below the surface. When upside down, the undercurrents are about to surface in an unpleasant way.

35.

Incomplete Actions
There is additional work or action required to bring your efforts to fruition. Portions remain incomplete for the required outcome. Inverted, portions have been omitted along the way.

36.

Assertiveness
Assertiveness is needed to bring about right action. It is time to be heard. If upside down, this rune indicates that overdue assertiveness could become aggression.

37.

Higher Learning
See behind the appearances
and recognize that you have
co-created this situation in
order to gain higher wisdom.
Upside down, you are taking the
situation at face value.

38.

The Inner Child
This rune advocates putting fun
and adventure into a situation for
best success. When inverted, an
unparented inner child of either
yourself or another is making the
decisions based on need.

39.

Greater Opportunities
This rune warns that something
insignificant looking could
lead to large and positive life
changes. Do not minimize paying
attention to the details. Upside
down, something seemingly
insignificant could lead to a very
large problem.

40.

Significant Events
A noteworthy event is about to
occur that requires recognition;
otherwise its gifts cannot be
reaped nor its lessons fully
understood.

41.

Accelerated Increase

If this rune is drawn regarding financial matters, expect rapid gains. It denotes increase in a positive way in whatever area of your life it is drawn in response to.

42.

Eagle Vision

This rune warns that a much larger perspective needs to be brought to bear on the situation. An eagle's perspective is necessary to see what's really going on. Observe indicators, but then step out of the situation for a clearer and larger view.

43.

Changing Perspective

It is now very important to look at things from a diametrically opposed viewpoint, or through another's eyes. Only then will you have the whole picture.

44.

Courage

Courage is needed to birth the greatness that lies dormant in the situation before you. Most decisions that are effective are huge, but require courage to implement over the long haul. When inverted, decisions are being ruled by fear.

45.

Fertility
The situation is fertile for opportunities to be born. Multiple outcomes lie before you.

46.

Healthy Boundaries
Drawing this rune is an indication that your boundaries need to be protected. Someone has encroached into areas of your life where they are drawing upon your resources without giving in return or without your permission.

47.

The Laws of Existence
The basic law of existence that must be considered when making a decision is that all must benefit equally from the outcome. At times this may mean severing a relationship so all may grow. Upside down, the web of existence has been damaged by someone acting in a self-centered way.

48.

Cataclysmic Change
Cataclysmic change is about to take place. When this rune is right side up, the change will lead to a higher order and beneficial results. Upside down indicates destruction.

49.

Obscured Vision
There is a portion of the situation that is temporarily obscured. That which is hidden from your sight will soon reveal itself through patience. Do not make decisions prematurely. Upside down, negativity is being hidden.

50.

Inner Mastery
This is a warning to make your decisions from your highest identity as a consciousness superimposed over all that is. Do not let your lowest fears determine your course of action.

51.

Shedding World Views
A radical departure from your normal way of seeing the world is required for opportunities in this situation to be maximized. Great truthfulness is required with yourself.

52.

Truth
This rune says that what is being portrayed is done so in truth. Upside down, beware – there is deceit. Make sure you are honest with yourself about your true feelings.

53.

Fluid Perception
It will be to your advantage to be
very fluid in changing directions
or courses of action, or to be
flexible with yourself and others.
Upside down, you or someone
else is being too rigid.

54.

Patience
Patience is advocated. The
desired results are going to
take longer than anticipated.
Upside down, it could mean that
someone's patience is wearing
thin or that you yourself are too
impatient about a situation.

55.

Credibility
When this rune is drawn in
response to a question about a
person or situation, you can be
sure they are believable. Upside
down however, there is an error
in what is being portrayed.

56.

Dependability
That which you are relying upon
is warranted. You can depend
either on the people involved or
the situation to live up to what it
represents.

57.

Balance

Balance is the pulsation between doingness and beingness; it does not mean equilibrium that is static. When overemphasis is given to either receptivity or proactivity, balance is disturbed.

58.

Strength

This is a time a show of strength is needed. It could be in the form of concerted effort, extra endurance, or assertive expression of your requirements. Upside down, strength is lacking in either yourself or others around you.

59.

Fruition

Your efforts are about to pay off. The seeds previously sown are on the verge of yielding their results. When inverted, effort will not come to full fruition.

60.

Prudence

Prudence in proceeding forward is advised. This rune indicates that you need to tread lightly; you are on delicate ground. If inverted, imprudent action has been taken.

61.

**Rebirth through
Self-regeneration**
Release old notions of yourself
and reshape yourself on your
eternal journey.

62.

Pleasure
This rune indicates that
pleasurable circumstances will
occur. Look forward with glad
anticipation.

63.

Vortex of Power
You have become a power point
and are drawing in auspicious
circumstances. This is the time to
envision your goals in great detail
to create positive results.

64.

Gestation
Nurture what has been begun
with tender care. This is a phase
of gestation when energy should
be put into the situation at hand.

65.

Expansion
This is the time to expand.
Make sure you have the
necessary resources at hand to
accommodate the expansion.
Expanded growth requires a firm
foundation. Upside down, it is
time to contract.

66.

Challenged Perception
It is time to turn gained
perception into experiential
knowledge. A time of testing
whether you live up to your
highest truth is at hand. When
inverted, unimpeccable actions
have taken place. Someone has
lived contrary to their highest
perception.

67.

Sparing Interaction
Either someone is not ready to
handle an abundance of your
energy and light, or your energy
could be drained by the situation.
Interact sparingly to avoid either.

68.

Justice
It is time for the scales to be
balanced. Either someone will
be brought to justice, or where
there has been more giving than
receiving, it will be time to
balance the books.

69.

Leadership

Leadership is required for events to go in the right direction. Either a leader should be appointed, or you need to assume responsibility for providing leadership. Upside down, poor leadership is being provided.

70.

Enthusiasm

Expect others to feel enthusiasm for what is being pondered and approach it with enthusiasm yourself.

71.

Shedding Expectations

It is very important to not base present expectations on past experience. This could damage beneficial outcome as well as relationships. Move forward unencumbered by baggage from the past.

72.

Friendship

Supportive friends and loyalty are before you. Nurture the relationships you may find in your environment.

73.

Innocence

Innocence requires living in the
moment. Don't try to anticipate
the future – let it come to you.
When upside down, someone has
an agenda.

74.

Effort

The perspective/relationship/
situation will require a great deal
of effort. Make sure the stakes
are worth fighting for. Upside
down, no amount of effort will
bring good results.

75.

Complexity

There is far more to this
than meets the eye. Unseen
involvement of other people or
factors will bring unpredictable
complexity. When inverted, there
is negative interference.

76.

Stoicism

Sometimes a period of gritting
one's teeth is required to get
through a tough spot. Upside
down, someone is not prepared to
see it through.

77.

Beauty
One cannot go wrong when drawing this rune. The beauty of the situation will be apparent to one with the eyes to see.

78.

Grace
The statement, "It would be easy if it were meant to be", is not always true. But in this case it is. The graceful flow of events will steer the course.

79.

Correction
There is something that needs to be fixed or changed. A correction needs to be made to put things back on track. Upside down, a flaw has produced adverse results. It could be a flaw of perception that must be corrected.

80.

Forgiveness
We are not required to allow those of low perception and intentions into our environment. We are required however, to see the perfection of life expressing at all levels, even as we let them go on their way. Upside down, someone is holding a grudge.

81.

Practical Details

We may have lofty dreams, but unless we tend to the practical details of their fulfillment, our dreams may not be realized. With this rune, be sure to attend to them.

82.

Exploration

The circumstances for which this rune is drawn will provide an exploration into aspects of life not yet encountered. When faced with what further to explore, let your feelings be your guide as to what is life-enhancing. Upside down, the exploration will lead to unpleasantness.

83.

The Calling

You are being called by the universe to fulfill a task for the enhancement of life. Do not sidestep that which is before you. It is in fulfilling our calling that life's possibilities open to us.

84.

The Good Omen

This rune assesses the overall benefits of the situation. This rune is helpful at times when we cannot see the forest for the trees. Depending on which side is up, this rune will indicate whether the pros outweigh the cons.

85.

The Crossroads
It is time to make a choice.
Divergent life choices lie
before you and can no longer
be ignored. It may be time for a
large life change. Upside down,
a change of direction and life
choice is overdue.

86.

Direction
This rune indicates that help is
at hand in defining what choice
to make. There will be markers
in your environment – pay close
attention. When inverted, you
should reassess – you are going
the wrong way.

87.

Chance Encounter
A person or situation that will
be very instrumental in your life
will be encountered. To receive
the gift this will bring, ask in
each situation, "What is the gift
this person or situation has for
me?" Upside down, someone
will attempt to draw you into
unpleasant circumstances.

88.

Elegant Solution
What may seem like a conflict or
dilemma has an elegant way of
being resolved that will enhance
the life of all involved. Being
aware of this will help it present
itself. Upside down, there is a
much better way to respond to
what is before you than the way
in which you intend or have
done.

89.

Enlightenment
A mundane situation holds within it the gift of insight that will change your life. Enlightenment will result. It is essential to see the perfection behind the appearances. Upside down, your vision is too superficial.

90.

The Unexpected
Be open and fluid, for an unexpected element will enter, creating a pleasant enhancement. Upside down, be prepared for an unexpected downturn of events. Once prepared, one has the luxury of expecting the best.

91.

Generosity
It is time to open your hands to give. Ask not whether the one before you is worthy of receiving the gift, for they are worthy of the greatest gift of all, which is life. There are key moments in the lives of others when your generosity could change the course of events.

92.

Infinite Perfection
What may seem like chaos is merely a lower order restructuring itself for a higher level of existence. Trust that the infinite perfection will reveal itself and endeavor to find it.

93.

The Power of Speech
Be very careful what words you choose. They may come back to haunt you. Reality is created thought by thought and word by word. Be respectful of all life through your words and know they contain the power of manifestation.

94.

The Sage
Take time to listen to your inner wisdom. Living a self-examined life creates character and depth. Also be aware of words of wisdom spoken by others in your environment – even those you usually regard as foolish.

95.

Creating Space
There is something in your life to which you need to give more time and attention. Don't let business crowd out what is important. Balance doingness with beingness and allow time for your inner child to be expressed and nurtured.

96.

Safeguarding the Sacred
Energy and awareness equate. The more energy you have, the more awareness is at your disposal and the more subtle, non-cognitive information you can access about the situation. This rune warns not to waste energy, for example on pacifying others.

The Seven Steps of Mastery

Step 4

The Three Keys of Knowledge – Mastering the Three Perspectives

Through insight does the heart change. When the heart changes, so does your world...

Almine

The Field of Perception of Mysticism

The Wheel for the Runes of the Field of Perception of Mysticism

Mysticism studies the hidden laws of existence so that we may create the graceful unfolding of our life by fully cooperating with them.

Shehere sarasach mines ekles virava
Suvet erekle misavich erenes subahit
Meste sereset krihunach etret priharavesvi
Akrava mestu hiruhach seresut estava

The impeccable spiritual warrior, in cooperation with divine will, walks the timeless journey in pristine power.

The Seven Perceptions of Mysticism help us understand the laws of Cosmic Life: through co-operating with the laws we may align ourselves with the power of the Cosmos.

The Three Equations of Formless Form

1.

2.

3.

The First Key of Knowledge

Question: When we leave the entrapment of mirrors, the sub-atomic particles (from which the mirrored life is fashioned) dissolve. Individuation occurs when these particles are clustered by frequency into form. What is the method by which individuation takes place when the sub-atomic particles (awareness particles) are eliminated?

Answer: The mind cannot grasp the matterless matter that is present when the sub-atomic particles disappear. The individual becomes a bright, blue-white ball of light that shines throughout the creative space. This occurs when the tensions of self-doubt, absent self-expression, and attachment to outcome as well as fear of your own vastness disappear.

The First Key of Knowledge

Equation of Formless Form 1

1.

The Building Blocks of Existence

Before February 2008

Sub-atomic particles of matter

Fused particles of love and light.

Presence particles

Separate frequency and light wave forms.

Life force particles

These particles differ from presence particles by an octave of frequency. They were Y-shaped.

Awareness particles

These look the way presence particles were supposed to look—a wobbly cross.

Love and Light particles

All building block particles had little separate pieces inter-mingled—left over from previous big bang explosions that ripped apart. These were separate wave forms.

Perception particles

These particles help perception to take place.

Self-perception particles (Mother took the creation of reality away from these particles). She took over this role on Feb. 12, 2008.

These particles were responsible for creating reality, the way a movie projector projects a movie.

(Figure 73)

The Second Key of Knowledge

Question: The evolution into matterless matter leaves the realities of the one and the many for a higher form of expression. Must we withdraw from the realities of opposites or attempt to dissolve them?

Answer: As the lightbearers of consciousness of this world, our reality may be intermingled with that of man, yet it is more highly evolved. When a child grows up too quickly, his or her innocence is disrupted. The illusion of the mirrored world formed from the sub-atomic particles is an incubation chamber for man to evolve within, at a comfortable pace. As the masters or elders of the world, we may neither abandon man, nor judge him for awakening from his childhood at his own pace. We may however shelter him within the luminosity of our presence.

The Second Key of Knowledge

Equation of Formless Form 2

2.

The Third Key of Knowledge

Question: What metamorphoses occurs in the body when we live in the fluid river of unfolding life? How does it affect the way our reality is shaped and experienced? How do others feel the effects of our presence?

Answer: As we enter the sixth field of perception, the field of godhood, structure becomes less rigid as we become the contradiction of life. In this stage fluid form becomes an embraced perspective. The more rigid form, especially of the first four perspectives, provided the external infrastructure through which inner expression can articulate. The possibilities in our reality flow fluidly and change comes exponentially if we live in surrendered trust.

The ida and pingala join and move as one in their spiral around the pranic tube. The inner language of the 672 senses (interpreted by the runes) speaks as a result of the whispering of Infinite Intent. It is then externally expressed. Because of the connection with Source in this sixth field of godhood, all are enriched through the graceful bestowal of resources from the one who has entered godhood.

In the seventh field of the unfolding journey, the pranic tube enlarges and encloses the merged ida and pingala. This stage can be described as super-godhood.

The Third Key of Knowledge

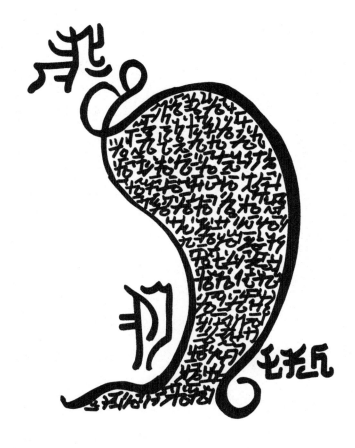

Equation of Formless Form 3

3.

The High Alchemy for the 20 Primary Meridians

Opening the Resurrection Points of the Navel and the High Heart

For as the High Heart opens, the black blood cells activate and the true interdimensional life begins.

Almine

The High Alchemy for the 20 Meridians to Open the Resurrection Points of the Navel and the High Heart

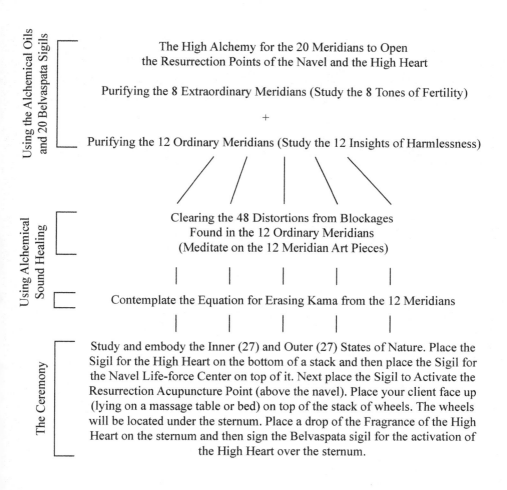

Using the Alchemical Oils and 20 Belvaspata Sigils

The High Alchemy for the 20 Meridians to Open
the Resurrection Points of the Navel and the High Heart

Purifying the 8 Extraordinary Meridians (Study the 8 Tones of Fertility)

+

Purifying the 12 Ordinary Meridians (Study the 12 Insights of Harmlessness)

Using Alchemical Sound Healing

Clearing the 48 Distortions from Blockages
Found in the 12 Ordinary Meridians
(Meditate on the 12 Meridian Art Pieces)

Contemplate the Equation for Erasing Kama from the 12 Meridians

The Ceremony

Study and embody the Inner (27) and Outer (27) States of Nature. Place the Sigil for the High Heart on the bottom of a stack and then place the Sigil for the Navel Life-force Center on top of it. Next place the Sigil to Activate the Resurrection Acupuncture Point (above the navel). Place your client face up (lying on a massage table or bed) on top of the stack of wheels. The wheels will be located under the sternum. Place a drop of the Fragrance of the High Heart on the sternum and then sign the Belvaspata sigil for the activation of the High Heart over the sternum.

It is highly recommended that those seeking entry into Master level, and especially Grand Master level of the Runes, be initiated first into the Belvaspata Healing modality. If you cannot do the Belvaspata level of the High Alchemy yourself, have a Belvaspata practitioner do it for you.

The Belvaspata sigils needed for the High Alchemy of the 20 Meridians are those of Mishba-Terasat, the Belvaspata for the Earth Heart connection (essential for the resurrection portal of the High Heart to open). For the Belvaspata portion of the meridian purification you will need to familiarize yourself with the 8 Tones of Fertility and the 12 Insights of Harmlessness.

Introduction to the 12 Insights of Harmlessness and the 8 Tones of Fertility

To restore the fluidity to the way in which we respond to life and the consequential fluid grace with which life unfolds, the old programmed blockages in the meridians must release.

The pre-requisite to releasing the blockages of the 12 meridians is the mastering of the 12 insights. The 8 Tones of Fertility clear the 8 Extraordinary meridians. The 12 meridians purify the experience of outer, spatial awareness. The 8 meridians purify inner space.

The Eight Tones of Fertility

Embody now the balance of the masculine and feminine, that which is receptive and pro-active simultaneously. In surrender let the automatic action express as inevitable deeds. Fertile shall the journey of this holy union be, when the song of your heart sings the eight tones.

Let these tones sing in your heart by becoming the surrendered interpreter of Infinite Intent. The inseminated birth of articulated potential shall fill the Earth with its newness and you shall shine as a great, white-blue star upon the Earth, bringing new hope to the sons of man and the new energy to all kingdoms.

Through combining the Eight Tones of Fertility with the Perspectives of the Seven Fields of Perception, the Master becomes the High Alchemist.

The Eight Tones of Fertility

1. Resonant awakening of the Opened Heart

2. The anticipated consummation of the eternal romance

3. The high alchemy of engaged participation

4. Mystical revelations of beckoning possibilities

5. Responsive stirrings of the senses as heralds of things to come

6. The fertile conception of perpetually regenerated creations

7. The hallowed marriage of the one and the many

8. The exciting expectation of the inspiration of unveiled mysteries.

The Twelve Insights of Harmlessness

1. For the Healing of the Lung Meridian

Angel: **Kribasach-huretvi**

Insight of Harmlessness: Transparent Truth

From the moment a lie is told, the whole cosmos conspires to reveal it. The nature of life is truth that flows in an unstoppable expression. An untruth is an attempt to obstruct the flow of life itself and must eventually fail in its pitiful effort to pit itself against Infinite expression in action.

2. For the Healing of the Large Intestine Meridian

Angel: **Mesenech-uplarasta**

Decisions of Empowerment

The only form of persecution to fear is self-persecution. Decisions based on protectiveness, persecute the self by denying its ability to manifest a life of unfolding grace and self-sovereign abundance. Protectiveness attracts persecution, whereas the self-sovereign confidence of the highest truth expressed mobilizes the support of the cosmos.

3. *For the Healing of the Stomach Meridian*

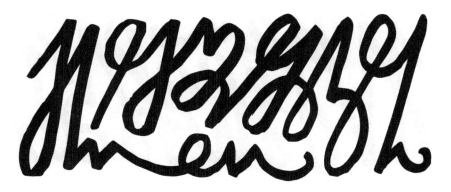

Angel: **Nensut-aravespi**

The Fluidity of Time

The past changes from the choices of the moment. But the past cannot change when we hold onto it in our memories, or when we have abandoned the moment. The moment only has the power to change the past and the future when our awareness is fully focused on it. When we live in the future or the past they become our tyrants.

4. For the Healing of the Spleen Meridian

Angel: **Krusanet-heratas**

Spontaneous Becoming

We encase ourselves in the rigid armor of our past stories. Driven by our need for continuity, we hold onto past stories, denying ourselves the fluid contribution of new vision. In releasing the desire for permanence, reference points and continuity, we release the constrictions of belief systems. Spontaneous becoming is then revealed bringing with it the gift of self-regeneration.

5. *For the Healing of the Heart Meridian*

Angel: **Arech-privahet**

Embracing Endlessness

Death is a result, not a cause. Its perceived tyranny is an illusion, since we are the first cause of anything that transpires in our reality. Death is the tool, the purification rite used by infinity to sweep clean the attempts to dam up the flow of eternal life with belief systems. When we release our identities and belief systems, the need for aging and death disappears as well.

6. For the Healing of the Small Intestine Meridian

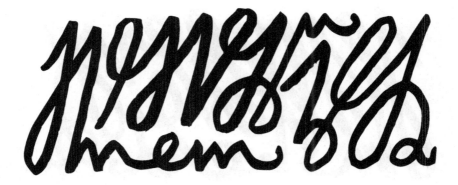

Angel: **Heleras-arsetu**

Endless Supply

The possibility of depletion and loss can no more exist than a hole can be made in the ocean. As soon as something is removed from our environment, something rushes in to take its place and fill the gap. When we are bereft of a loved one, we cannot imagine that anything could compensate for it. Yet the loved one has at some level volunteered to provide us with the opportunity to gain strength, depth and other valuable gifts from the experience.

7. For the Healing of the Bladder Meridian

Angel: **Hansak-brivates**

Comfort with the Eternal Journey

We are challenged to move beyond the boundaries of our comfort zones by the more enlightened, as well as the less enlightened in our environment. The master and the fool thus serve the same purpose of helping us transcend our existing paradigms and evolve our interpretive expression of our part in the Infinite's design. In embracing whatever form our challenge to expand our horizons comes in, our comfort with the eternal journey grows. Our confidence in our ability to meet the challenges of life deepens.

8. For the Healing of the Kidney Meridian

Angel: **Menserech-karsatu**

The Self-examined Life

When we see others in life stagger and fall under burdens and challenges, we could be led to deduce that there are some situations we are not equipped to cope with. But for every challenge we face, we have what it takes to surmount it. Even if it feels as though our hearts have broken and our life lies in ashes, the eternal aspect rises again like spring grass in a blackened field. Painful challenges come to awaken those unused qualities and unexpressed strengths we hide in false humility. To push our limits, and stretch our wings slightly each day, makes forced change unnecessary, yielding instead to graceful change.

9. For the Healing of the Pericardium Meridian

Rachve-minut-haras

Angel: **Nenerach-hirsetvavu**

Choosing our Reality

We have misunderstood our role in manifesting opposition in our lives. Because it seemed that some external force was inflicting the hardships, we rationalized what else would seem out of our control. We called it 'an unescapable part of life.' We gave it the noble purpose of testing and shaping us. Although gaining its insights, once we are in the midst of hardship, is the most expedient way not to have to repeat it, it is by no means a necessary way to learn. Living in full awareness, to change perception fluidly in the moment, can achieve the same impetus to move with grace in the infinite dance of existence.

10. For the Healing of the Thyroid Meridian

Angel: **Kuhuravek-blivabech**

Creative Contribution through Emphases

In certain religions the devil, representing evil, is elevated to the status of being the opposite of the Infinite. The same inconceivable over-valuing of evil is done by many who fear it, protect against it, and worry about it entering the lives of themselves or their loved ones. It is this misperception that empowers it and makes it come alive, as though worrying about your shadow can bring it to life. To turn on the light, banishes shadows. Remove your focus from perceived evil; find what within yourself you are not accepting, and focus on living to the fullest of your heart's content. Be generous with yourself in supporting the song of your heart.

11. For the Healing of the Gall Bladder Meridian

Angel: **Haranach-sersatu**

Miracles through Surrendered Trust

The true meaning of humility is an approach to life that acknowledges the unknowable nature of existence, but embraces it with a surrendered trust. Trust stems from the knowing that the manifestation of Infinite Intent comes in the form of subtle promptings that you are able to interpret through effortless cooperation with life. In complete oneness with Infinite Intent, the mind empties of old knowledge and the heart opens to new possibilities.

12. For the Healing of the Liver Meridian

Angel: **Rakvravis-perspatur**

Immaculate Timing

Life unfolds with immaculate timing, even if we imagine that in some way we may have missed a chance, been too late or too premature. Like the perfection of a spider web, in which each thread is dependent on every other thread, timing affects trillions of other events and jointly creates an expression of Infinite Intent. We may wish for something to have unfolded differently, and think its timing to be flawed, but in trust we can feel what only a larger perspective can reveal: the absolute perfect purpose behind every event.

The Use of Fragrance Alchemy Oil to Clear the Eight Extraordinary Meridians of the Body

The Polluted Rivers of Old Memories

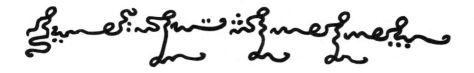

Purify the eight ways in which memories are retained through perception, and then purify the 12 ordinary meridians with alchemical oils on the acupressure points. Follow this with the Belvaspata protocol for the 20 meridians.

Introduction

It has long baffled sincere light-seekers that no matter how much self-work they have done, it seems as though old memories keep resurfacing to disrupt their emotional equilibrium.

Memories have been held in the magnetic fields of the body, generated by the 20 meridians of the body, and specifically by the eight extraordinary meridians themselves. The application of the alchemical oils on the meridians' acupressure points helps to facilitate the release and removal of these blockages that obstruct the flow of life force and eventually cause physical injuries and disease.

The Eight Ways in Which Memories are Kept

1. Cellular Memory: The function has been to place short-term memories into long-term memory patterns. Memories are held in the membrane around the nucleus.

2. Instinctual Memory: Emergency responses are held in the 3rd chakra.

3. Racial Memory: Stored in the chakra located a hand's length into the ground, beneath your feet. Racial memories determine danger assessment.

4. Membranes between Realities: Held in the psoas muscle. Keeps memories of passages between life, death and ascension and awake and dream states.

5. Membranes of the eye and optic nerve: Remember what has been seen.

6. Membranes of the ears: Remember what has been heard.

7. Taste buds: Remember value judgements of good and bad.

8. All hair on the skin: Holds memories of extra-sensory experiences; that which happens out of range of perception.

    The sense of smell never fell into duality
    Let fragrant oils heal the storage of old memories

From the Ancient Alchemical Texts

The accumulated memories burdensome became
From clustered information, blocked meridians came
Eight alchemical oils of which we tell
The eight meridians' illusions and debris dispel

The Meridians and The Eight Alchemical Oils

1. Ren Mai Meridian   Arabian Nights Blend
    Dispels the illusion of activity / inactivity

2. Yin Qiao Mai Meridian   Blue Lagoon Blend
    Dispels the illusion of permanence / transience

3. Du Mai Meridian   Lily Blend
    Dispels the illusion of life enhancing / non-lifeenhancing

4. Yang Qiao Mai Meridian   Luxor Blend
    Dispels the illusion of hidden / evident

5. Chong Mai Meridian   Papyrus Blend
    Dispels the illusion of individual choice / Infinite intent

6. Yin Wei Mai Meridian   Magnolia Blend
    Dispels the illusion of inner / outer

7. Dai Mai Meridian   Hathor Blend
    Dispels the illusion of past / present

8. Yang Wei Mai Meridian   Secret of Nefertiti Blend
    Dispels the illusion of individuation / oneness

Through the illusion of opposites, illness did come

The Equations to Heal Duality with the Alchemical Oils
(www.fragrancealchemy.com)

Using the Equations of the Alchemical Oils

Prior to treating a meridian, you can look at and read the equation or you may wish to run your finger or fingers across the lines of the equation (from left to right) before applying the oil. When running your finger across the equation, you may use either hand – the left hand being receptive and the right hand representing understanding.

When storing the oils, the bottles may be placed on the equations. Laminating will help to protect them.

Arabian Nights Blend

The removal of the illusion of activity
and inactivity

+

The integrated oneness of the observer and
the observed

=

The evolved expression of awareness

Blue Lagoon Blend

The eternal perspective of knowing there is neither
permanance nor transcience

+

The recognition of the deep peace of the eternal
fluid moment

=

Becoming the contradiction of the perpetual
regeneration of the eternal self

Lily Blend

Releasing the illusion of life enhancing and
non-life enhancing

+

The fluid regeneration of life without the
illusion of beginnings and endings

=

Surrendered trust in the mutually supportive
nature of existence

Luxor Blend

The healing of value judgements through seeing
the hidden revealed in the obvious

+

Polarity as the tool to create the fluid form of
Infinite intent

=

Purity in action through participation with the Infinite's
design as revealed through effortless knowing

Papyrus Blend

The realization that individual choice and
Infinite Intent are one

+

Individual responses evoked by the inspiration
of Infinite Intent

=

The timeless artistry of Source in
diverse expressions

Magnolia Blend

The awakening of the magic life through the merging of
inner and outer realities

+

The innocent existence of releasing judgements and
programmed expectations

=

Resonant responsiveness to the Source of our
inspiration by living from the quantum field
of tonal luminousity

Hathor Blend

The dissolving of the illusion that any part of existence
is excluded from the newness of Infinite expression

+

Accessing the rapture of the all-pervading presence
of the Infinite

=

Knowing the stillness-in-motion of the standing
waveform of exponential time

Secret of Nefertiti Blend

Individuation as a tool of Oneness to create constriction so
as to build momentum for perceptual motion

+

Reverence for all beings as manifested expressions
of the One Life

=

Knowing the potency of our existence as an archetypal
expression to be a unique aspect of the One Being

Using the Fragrant Oils to Clear Memories

Apply the oils to the specific acupressure points as indicated on the illustrations that follow. Massage the oil in small clockwise circles. Massaging the oil can be done for just a few seconds, as the primary element is the fragrance on the meridian point.

When applying the oil to the 8 extraordinary meridians, the oil is applied to **two** points (the master point and the coupling point) for each meridian.

The 8 Extraordinary Meridians and the Fragrant Oil

1. Ren Mai Meridian   Arabian Nights Blend

2. Yin Qiao Mai Meridian   Blue Lagoon Blend

3. Du Mai Meridian   Lily Blend

4. Yang Qiao Mai Meridian   Luxor Blend

5. Chong Mai Meridian   Papyrus Blend

6. Yin Wei Mai Meridian   Magnolia Blend

7. Dai Mai Meridian   Hathor Blend

8. Yang Wei Mai Meridian   Secret of Nefertiti Blend

The Eight Extraordinary Meridians
(Apply the oil to both the master point and the coupling point)

For each of the extraordinary meridians, when treating **men**, apply the oil to the master point on the **left** side of the body first, and then apply the oil to the coupling point on the **right** side of the body.

For **women** apply the oil to the master point on the **right** side of the body first, and then apply the oil to the coupling point on the **left** side of the body.

1. Ren Mai   Arabian Nights Blend

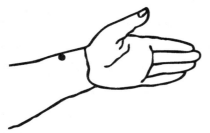   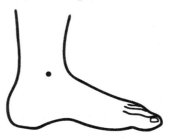

Master Point   Coupling Point

2. Yin Qiao Mai   Blue Lagoon Blend

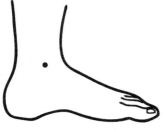   

Master Point   Coupling Point

3. Du Mai

Master Point

Lily Blend

Coupling Point

4. Yang Qiao Mai

Master Point

Luxor Blend

Coupling Point

5. Chong Mai

Papyrus Blend

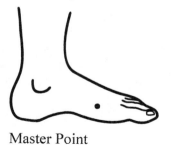

Master Point

Coupling Point

6. Yin Wie Mai

Magnolia Blend

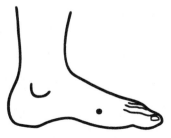

Master Point

Coupling Point

7. Dai Mai

Hathor Blend

Master Point

Coupling Point

8. Yang Wie Mai

Secret of Nefertiti Blend

Master Point

Coupling Point

The Use of Fragrance Alchemy Oil to Clear the Twelve Meridians of the Body

Note: The Fragrance Alchemy oils and instructions for their use are available at http://alminewisdom.com/collections/fragrance-alchemy.

The Fragrant Oil Formula for the Lung Meridian

The Neroli Blend
(3:00 am – 5:00 am)

+

+

=

Massage the oil on the meridian point as indicated. Depending on the aspect of the emotion, place the oil on the right side of the body for a positive aspect, the left side for a negative aspect and either side for a neutral aspect.

The Fragrant Oil Formula for the Large Intestine Meridian

The Jasmine Blend
(5:00 am – 7:00 am)

+

+

=

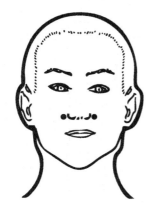
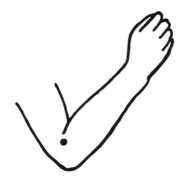

243

The Fragrant Oil Formula for the Stomach Meridian

The Sandalwood Blend
(7:00 am – 9:00 am)

+

+

=

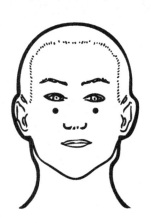

The Fragrant Oil Formula for the Spleen Meridian

The Fuchsia Blend
(9:00 am – 11:00 am)

The Fragrant Oil Formula for the Heart Meridian

The Rose Blend

(11:00 am – 1:00 pm)

The Fragrant Oil Formula for the Small Intestine Meridian

The Lotus Blend

(1:00 pm – 3:00 pm)

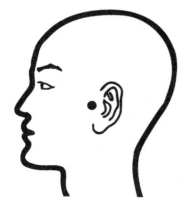

The Fragrant Oil Formula for the Bladder Meridian

The Saffron Blend
(3:00 pm – 5:00 pm)

+

+

=

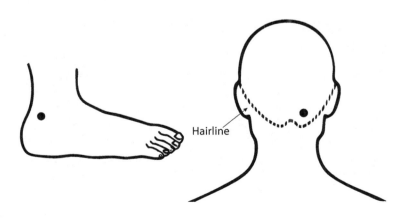

Hairline

The Fragrant Oil Formula for the Kidney Meridian

The Narcissus Blend

(5:00 pm – 7:00 pm)

+

+

=

Behind the knee and on the inner aspect of the leg .

The Fragrant Oil Formula for the Pericardium/ Circulation Meridian

The Henna Blend

(7:00 pm – 9:00 pm)

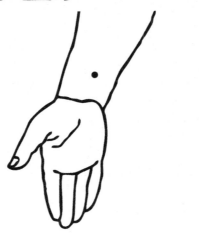

The Fragrant Oil Formula for the Thyroid Meridian

The Oud Blend
(9:00 pm – 11:00 pm)

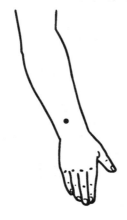

251

The Fragrant Oil Formula for the Gallbladder Meridian

The Patchouli Blend

(11:00 pm – 1:00 am)

+

+

=

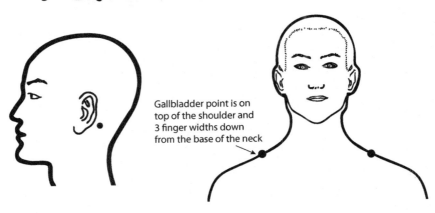

Gallbladder point is on top of the shoulder and 3 finger widths down from the base of the neck

The Fragrant Oil Formula for the Liver Meridian

The Gardenia Blend

(1:00 am – 3:00 am)

Meridian Instructions

To change the cellular matrix to the higher evolution of expression and activate godhood in the individual, the removal of blockages in the 12 main meridians of the body is essential. The blockages are the origin of memory, linear time, and the negative emotions associated with them. Fragrance, as the one sense that never fell (its frequency remained high), is a key component in providing an effortless solution to blockages caused by separation consciousness, reminding the body of its oneness with Source.

The booklet that accompanies the set of twelve fragrances for the specific meridians, indicates the acupressure points onto which the oils should be massaged. When treating yourself or another, massage the oil in small clockwise circles. The massaging can be done just for a few seconds, as the primary element is the fragrance on the meridian point, and not the massaging. The bottoms of the feet are the most receptive area for the placement of oils and they can be placed there before bedtime or if the fragrance is not something you wish to be noticed (men may not want to smell of a feminine fragrance). Inside shoes and socks, the fragrances are hardly detectable.

There are multiple acupressure points for each meridian that can be found online. The ones indicated in the booklet were chosen based on their accessibility when treating a client. Please note the thyroid meridian could also be called the Triple Warmer meridian.

Note: The negative aspect of an emotion indicates those parts of the emotion that are suppressed. The neutral aspect indicates what is frozen and blocked by others or circumstances. The positive aspect indicates what is acted out or expressed. Depending on the aspect of the emotion, place the oil on the right side of the body for a positive aspect, the left side for a negative aspect and either side for a neutral aspect.

The 20 Belvaspata Sigils for Healing Early Developmental Trauma

1.

Mechpa-suvihanat

Angel: *Bisherevespi-asanat*

2.

Sehut-ublisvi

Angel: *Mesenet-selevit*

3.

Kirsana-sevehetvi

Angel: *Meste-nenuvis*

4.

Selvahut-arsaba   Angel: *Mispech-bilavespi*

5.

Sihat-kilinesvi   Angel: *Kasana-sivavet*

6.

Sihach-isanatvi   Angel: *Kelsi-aras-irastavi*

7.

Mananach-sehevavi   Angel: *Kisatra-bilavespi*

8.

Neneskar-siklavi

Angel: *Bisaret-nenkla*

9.

Pirarat-araves

Angel: *Sekla-heruhit*

10.

Parspanut-esevi

Angel: *Akra-subavit*

11.

Karsava-nechspi

Angel: *Klisaret-perenur*

12.

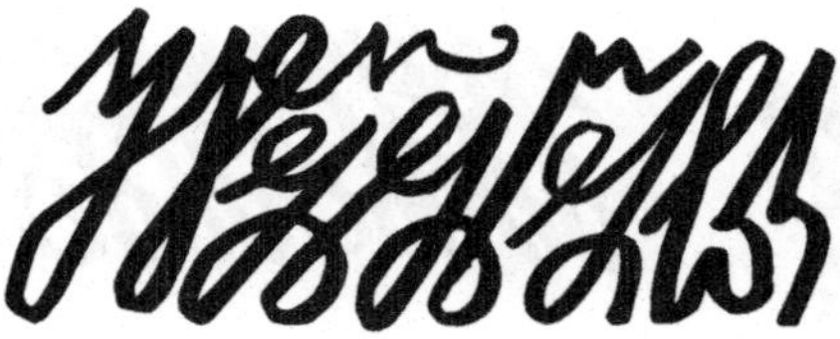

Triharasa-mesetre

Angel: *Esanich-visenat*

13.

Kesva-nenesta

Angel: *Piravit-aranas*

14.

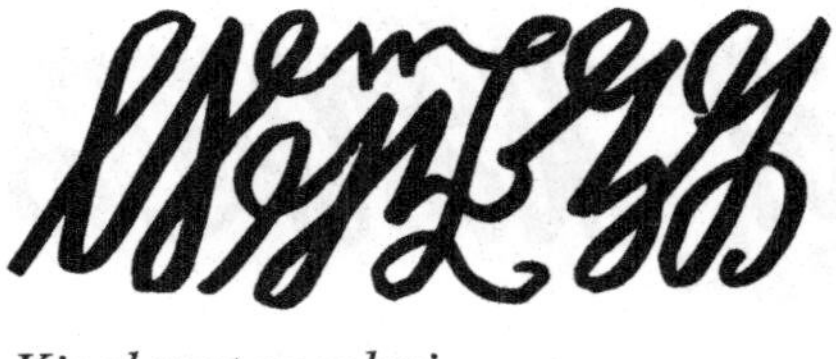

Kisalavet-mechpi

Angel: *Mechnet-herevesvi*

15.

Estra-birarek

Angel: *Mistre-husparek*

16.

Mirechtu-nenesva

Angel: *Sivet-arestu*

17.

Misenechvi-selvatut

Angel: *Bichpa-sevahat*

18.

Kelspa-rachnavet   Angel: *Helsat-ukresve*

19.

Kerseta-ublichvi   Angel: *Bichspa-urespi*

20.

Sihut-satve-minuhet   Angel: *Karas-uherevespa*

See Belvaspata Angel Healing Volumes 1-3 at https://www.
spiritualjourneys.com for general practice guidelines and all
information regarding the use of this angelic healing modality of light
and frequency.

Closing Sigils

Praise

Love

Gratitude

Sound Healing for the 12 Meridians of the Body

The Twelve Meridians and their Physical Functions

The 48 Sound Healing Elixirs plus the Resolution Elixir are designed to dissolve and release emotions as they surface for healing. Check this page for their availability: http://www.alminewisdom.com/12-meridians.

The twelve Ordinary Meridians can be divided into four categories representing the four directions. These categories describe the origin of blockages and the consequent dysfunction that results in the body and emotions.

Each meridian produces four different perspectives that appear as an emphasis in each person's life. For this reason, a blocked lung meridian for example, would produce grief for one person and intolerance in another person, and so forth. The perspective that each person adopts is based on the emphases of the qualities of a specific direction in his or her life.

Category 1

The Meridians of the Physical (representing the direction of the South)

1. The Lung Meridian
    For treatment of the lungs, breathing, skin, throat and neck.

2. The Pericardium Meridian
    Regulates the heart, opens the chest, stops pain, heart pain, agitation and restlessness.

3. The Heart Meridian
    Calms, stimulates the brain, invigorates the blood, regulates heart energy.

Category 2

The Meridians of the Soul (representing the direction of the West)

1. The Liver Meridian
   Benefits eyes and muscles, eliminates stagnation and invigorates the blood.

2. The Gallbladder Meridian
   Assists with imbalances in the gallbladder and relaxes the diaphragm.

3. The Stomach Meridian
   Resolves phlegm and damp; stimulates digestive abilities.

Category 3

The Meridians of the Lower Spirit (representing the direction of the East)

1. The Spleen Meridian
   Assists in stimulating the lower abdomen or epigastrium; clears spleen prolapse and harmonizes the spleen and liver functions.

2. The Kidney Meridian
   Clears imbalances in the kidneys, including heat and dampness.

3. The Large Intestine Meridian
   Regulates the large intestine and stops diarrhea and pain.

Category 4

The Meridians of the Higher Spirit (representing the direction of the North)

1. The Thyroid (Tripe Warmer) Meridian

Opens water passages and stimulates the transportation of fluids in the body.

2. The Small Intestine Meridian
    Tones the kidneys and benefits urination; assists with urinary retention or blood in the urine. Assists with managing diarrhea, blood and mucous in the stool, constipation, and abdominal pain.

3. The Bladder Meridian
    Eliminates stagnation and masses in the lower water passages. It addresses lower back pain, swelling and ulcers of the genitals.

Overall Higher Purposes of Clearing the Twelve Ordinary Meridians

- The goal of higher spiritual evolution is the combined expression of inner and outer space. The pure and unimpeded flow of resources along the passages of the twelve ordinary meridians helps dissolve barriers to inner space.
- Harmonious interaction of purified meridians clears the trauma held in the body's organs and supports the organs by forming a holistic and unified field.
- The 12 ordinary meridians help organize life within the matrix of man in order to release the necessary power to transcend linear change by replacing it with exponential change.
- Each person emits a unique frequency, called the "Song of the Self", because of his or her unique perspective. The pure functioning of the 12 meridians increases serotonin production, which emphasizes and enhances the individual's expression of his signature song, emitted at a cellular level.
- There are a total of 672 unique points on the 12 meridians – 56 points on each meridian. There are 672 acupuncture points on the skin. The proper functioning of the meridians therefore, enhances

the opening and full expression of the little energy vortices: the acupuncture points. This activates a second support system of bodily health and emotional well-being.

- There are 672 inner senses and 7 external senses (including the skin's response to the environment without being touched, and the visceral response of the organs). The ability to communicate between the inner and outer sensory responses lies in the bridges between the inner and outer space: the 12 meridians.

- The higher functions of the 12 meridians include the activation of a third blood cell: the black blood cell. Indigenous and magical traditions in many geographical locations have held the long lost knowledge of these cells that appear as little vortices, and as with all black light are not visible to the human eye. An example of this is the mystic's cord: a braid made of 3 white cords, 3 red cords and 3 black cords braided together.

- Without the vital role of the 12 meridians in the production of the black blood cells, the evolved expression of higher pheromones cannot take place. The one in ego-identification emits sexual pheromones, which in duality are designed for the survival of the species through procreation. The next level of unique, individual expression through evolved pheromones broadcasts an interpretation of Infinite Intent. These pheromones are called 'God hormones'. The third level of pheromone communication with the environment comes from the black blood cells of an advanced resurrected being. It carries messages of the manifestation of Divine Will.

- The advanced hormonal messages are the language of Infinite Intent, uniting oneness and polarity, and restoring the memory of the indivisibility of life. When we secrete them, we become catalysts for others: a key to prepare the environment and to accelerate the ability of others to transcend the programming of the world. As we are able to emit higher hormones that cross all barriers, we resonate in all levels at once, uniting oneness and polarity. Evolved hormones are the language of the Infinite.

The Meridian Clock

The Meridian Clock maps out the most beneficial times to treat the 12 meridians during a 24-hour cycle. Each meridian has a two-hour period during which its receptivity and proactivity are emphasized. The clock delineates which meridian system is dominant at a specific time, in order that its treatment may be more efficient.

The Clock

1. Lung Meridian: 3:00 am – 5:00 am
2. Large Intestine Meridian: 5:00 am –7:00 am
3. Stomach Meridian: 7:00 am – 9:00 am
4. Spleen Meridian: 9:00 am – 11:00 am
5. Heart Meridian: 11:00 am – 1:00 pm
6. Small Intestine Meridian: 1:00 pm – 3:00 pm
7. Bladder Meridian: 3:00 pm – 5:00 pm
8. Kidney Meridian: 5:00 pm – 7:00 pm
9. Pericardium Meridian: 7:00 pm – 9:00 pm
10. Thyroid Meridian: 9:00 pm – 11:00 pm
11. Gallbladder Meridian: 11:00 pm – 1:00 am
12. Liver Meridian: 1:00 am – 3:00 am

The Use of Sound Healing for the 12 Meridians

Belief systems are the tools of someone's worldview trying to exert its point of view onto the environment. From the belief systems come our personal identities. As the body holds these programs, the resources flowing through the meridians are impeded. The fake realities we make through our beliefs are held in geometrical structures of light within these energetic channels.

Light trapped within geometry also binds energy that becomes inaccessible to the individual, resulting in decay and ill health. Once these old programs release, energy is again made available, enabling increased perception and consciousness.

The distorted frequencies that result from blockages in a meridian, such as fear, rage, pain and protectiveness, are like a piano note that is held beyond its time to play. Captured by the geometry of belief systems, the frequencies of yesterday are unable to go through the graceful changes of the unfolding river of eternal existence. Like a dam across the river, these blockages cause stagnation, and this in turn invites forced changes through hardship and opposition.

The shattering of the emotional and mental blockages can come through intense emotional changes or perception that transcends the boundaries of existing paradigms. In the same way that a large earthquake can cause far more discomfort than multiple small shifts in the tectonic plates, sound healing can dissolve blockages in a far more subtle and gentle way.

The methods employed by sound healing fall into two categories:
- Firstly, it could use black sound balanced with white sound in order to remove illusion. This tackles the illusions trapped in the blockage directly.
- Secondly, it could create a strong enough set of tones that articulate the higher frequencies of a master. This can create a higher resonance in the blockage by altering the old trapped frequencies, and thereby dissolve the imprisoning geometries.

In the 48 sound healing musical pieces, both methods are used, depending on what needs to be addressed. As the old releases, negative emotions will surface that may at times cause some discomfort. The resolution piece is designed to assist with this. Its sole purpose is to remind us through frequency, that separation never has been anything more than illusion: that in forgetting our connection with all life, we created our own matrices of suffering.

Please note:
The 12 Meridian Light Elixirs are masterfully produced using the alchemical potentices of light to dispel the geometric belief systems that block the meridians. Meditate on them while listening to the Resolution Sound Elixir.

The Equation for Erasing Karma from the 12 Meridians

The Lung Meridian

1. Grief

Patterns of old perceptions, trapping negative emotions such as grief, form blockages in the meridian. This manifests as karma: the result of regrets. Regrets dissolve when the wholeness of life is remembered.

+

2. Intolerance

When life is seen as whole, we accept the lesser contribution of others who, as the buds on the rosebush, have not blossomed into full flowering of consciousness. Intolerance disappears as we accept the contribution of diversity.

+

3. Frustration

Frustration is felt when we try and control the speed at which outcomes manifest. The obstructions of life are timing mechanisms needed when we lose contact with the natural rhythms of the flow of rest and activity.

+

4. Bitterness

By trusting and relaxing into the flow of life, its artistry can be seen. That which we regard as hardships serves as much of a purpose as the times of peace. In knowing that through awareness and surrender we can increase graceful change, bitterness is replaced by poise.

=

Through releasing the fear of not making the right choices, or taking the right actions, clarity is restored. Authenticity unfolds and the journey of life becomes a graceful one.

The Large Intestine Meridian

1. Guilt
There is no foundation for the shortsighted perception that a mistake can be made, when one assesses it from an eternal perspective. The fluid map of time represents the Infinite's intent within cosmic life. Whatever direction we choose over the eons, will prove to be innocent. There is only the Infinite's will. Our freedom of choice merely is which of the paths we wish to explore.

+

2. Disappointment
All disappointment is self-made and stems from valuing the outcome more than the quality of the journey. Attachment to outcome can be described as the folly of attempting to dam up the raging river of life. A controlled outcome prohibits miracles from achieving results beyond our expectation. Expect miracles, hold on loosely to your desires and enjoy the never-ending journey of existence.

+

3. Remorse
Whether our chosen journey leads through light or through shadow, there is no right or wrong choice. Within the great pattern of existence, all is innocent when seen from an eternal perspective.

+

4. Opposition to Change

When spontaneity is missing from our lives, we become addicted to predictability. Addiction is always the result of suppressed expression. The false comfort of stagnation in the dam of the known will eventually be forced to yield to the river of change. When we allow it to happen, life changes gracefully, rather than forcefully.

=

The self-guided journey is one of inner strength and self-sovereignty. The aspects of life that we can self-determine are our responses to what lies before us, and what we choose to be inspired by. It is through our inspiration that we are guided, rather than through the forced changed of our hardships.

The Stomach Meridian

1. Disgust

It is from the self-imagined standards of what is acceptable and what is not, that our disgust and disdain is born. Disgust cannot exist in the life of one who is self-accepting. In a lack of self-love, does one externalize as an object of disgust, the components of yourself that you do not accept.

+

2. Greed

In the illusion of limited supply and lack, do the seeds of greed sprout. The moment is like a treasure chest, containing all that one needs to live it gloriously. It is only for the unaware that it seems lacking. We are part of nature and all of nature is bounteous in its supply and endless expression.

+

3. Shame

In our hearts lingers the long-lost promise that our destiny and capabilities are so much more than they seem. This creates the feeling of inadequacy, failure and shame. But during cosmic cycles of day and night, there are times of sleep and awakening. These are part of the eternal symphony of the Infinite, and the level at which we are able to express is but part of the music.

+

4. Blame

Through our lack of self-worth, we build ourself up by reducing and blaming others. Shame, when turned outward, becomes blame. Let us acknowledge that in the unfathomable pattern of life's grand design, every life has equal worth. We can only honor, but not dictate, the choices of others.

=

Intolerance for others can be replaced by a mindset that searches for inspiration in the daily encounters of life. Unsung heroes are found everywhere because, unlike physical courage, moral courage goes unseen. To find the beauty of life as an unfolding work of art requires the still poise of a master, who is able to see behind the appearances.

The Spleen Meridian

1. Worry

Worrying is a self-destructive act, because it attracts the negative outcome that it is concerned about. Knowing that our being is our sustenance, we can live in the moment, secure in the knowledge that we are the one at the helm of the reality we navigate. The future is created in the moment. If we abandon the moment to concern ourselves with the future, the future is haphazardly formed, rather than masterfully, by living the moment well.

+

2. Anxiety about the Future

The future is the unknown; the present seems to be the known. Mind, and its assistants reason and intelligence, prefer the known to the unknown. But the known is not really known at all; it is rather a momentary snapshot of the changing face of the river of eternity. If we accept that nothing can be truly known, for in a moment it has already changed, then we can also come to terms with the unavoidable fact that all is a limitless ocean – an incomprehensible expression of the Infinite One.

+

3. Self-destructiveness

Through self-reflection, do we imagine our unworthiness. When we deem ourselves unworthy of success, we self-sabotage our achievements. If we unselfconsciously and authentically express our highest truth, the result will always be self-supportive.

+

4. Mood Swings

It is in finding enjoyment in the little things of life, through aware appreciation of the details, that our mood extremes become balanced. The joy of the mundane allows us to have a stable platform from which to explore the valleys and the hills of our responses to life.

=

Through our aware appreciation, life flourishes in our environment. Through self-appreciation, the inner conflicts of obsolete programs yield to self-supported peace and contentment.

The Heart Meridian

1. Joylessness

Joy is restored by the expression of authentic desires of the self-fulfilled heart. Joy is found through optimizing the possibilities of the moment. It is the unconditional wonderment at the revelation of the Divine in expression through individuated life.

+

2. Anger

Anger is the desire to change that which is seen to block evolution or progress. The realization that nothing can be 'cleared' without moving it simply to another place, only to be encountered later, can inspire us to use a different tool than anger. Anger can break up stuck or stagnant areas of life, but unless we then replace it with the new perception this makes available, anger becomes destructive.

+

3. Self-pity

The masses living in duality are steeped in self-pity because of the nature of a reality in which opposites are self-pillaging. For instance, more day is less night. Furthermore, according to the law of compensation, there is always a price to pay for flourishing. The stage of duality is but a stepping stone to the stages beyond and serves the purpose of strengthening and refining the experience of individuation.

+

4. Neediness

The distorted perspective that there can be loss or lack, discounts the profound ability of an individual to affect his environment with a change of attitude. You are the master artist, chiseling the contours of your life.

=

The decision to live a life of mastery of mind and self-sovereignty of emotional needs is a large one, like deciding to build a temple. The bricks however, have to be laid one shining moment at a time.

Small Intestine Meridian

1. Insecurity

When someone in our environment becomes dominant, others tend to defer to that person. Certainty is not the equivalent of accuracy and it is usually the more enlightened one that admits he does not know. Be secure in the awareness that no one is insignificant in the intricate design of life. Remove one strand from a spiderweb and it is weakened and incomplete.

+

2. Sadness

Sadness arises when we believe that beneficial change is impossible and suffering is inevitable. Life changes from moment to moment, rewriting itself in discernable ways. Because complete reality shifts have no frame of reference we can use to measure them by, encouraging changes cannot be seen but have to be trusted. In this way, we become the visionholders of the world.

+

3. Abandonment

Most distorted programs in the meridians can be eliminated by the dynamic and balanced expression of the inner sub-personalities: the inner child, inner nurturer, inner sage and inner warrior. When the inner child is expressed and nurtured by its inner family, it can never feel abandoned. The feeling of abandonment is always preceded by self-abandonment.

+

4. Feeling Unheard
The ability to be heard is dependent on our listening to our own inner needs, desires and promptings. Not heeding the intuitive and non-cognitive communications within reflects outwardly into our interactions with others. When speaking your truth, do not expect to be understood. Only a master without a dialogue of the mind can hear you, but the universe is listening and will respond.

=

Acknowledge with gratitude the support of the universe, for that which receives gratitude increases. As an expression of Infinite life, you do not need to justify your existence. You complete the picture of the artistry of life in your own unique way.

The Bladder Meridian

1. Fright and Shock
The most debilitating affect of fright and shock is the tremendous loss of energy that takes place when it occurs. To prevent this, completely clear the mind, for if emergency action is required, an empty mind will ensure that an automatic response takes place.

2. Impatience
Rapid expectations of how the timing of unfolding events should occur, as well as how events should unfold, create impatience. The result is increased tension in the body, which keeps it in a state of density. Many deliberately create tense situations so that they can maintain an addiction to density. This keeps them from experiencing

fear of their vastness. The solution for this is the knowledge that
we are a being as vast as the cosmos, having a human experience; a
consciousness superimposed over all that is.

+

3. Restlessness
Restlessness results from an imbalance between the receptive and
proactive aspects within. Neither the imbalance of excess beingness
nor the excess of doingness, promotes the proper flow of energy
needed for the continual evolution of consciousness. The one causes
stagnation and the other, a leakage of energy. The realization that
one's value lies as much in who they are as in what they do, helps to
bring balance. It is necessary to remind ourselves that the emergency
mode of restlessness that we carry through our day is self-made and
unnecessary.

+

4. Unfulfillment
Divine discontent is within all creatures: in the plant reaching for
the sun, the migration of animals and birds, and the baby reaching
for its mother. When it draws us out of the moment, it becomes an
impediment to self-actualization of available potential. When it is
used as a reminder that life is an adventure to be explored, it can assist
in preventing the stagnation of complacency. Hear its voice, but do
not obsess about it. Focus instead on the fulfillment that is available.

=

Upon the many roads of Infinite intent, the individual may choose
which one he wishes to travel on. Unless he listens to the inspired
guidance of the heart, the journey will be determined by the forced,
and often traumatic, prodding of life. The self-sovereign acceptance

that our life can unfold with grace when inspired, provides a beacon of hope on the eternal journey.

The Kidney Meridians

1. Fear

Fear is a stranger to one who has embraced the knowledge that we live in an unknowable universe; that what we think we know changes constantly in unseen ways. Fear is born of the mind's desire to control, by labeling everything. It signals that we have encountered an area of our life that we have not yet embraced in surrendered trust.

+

2. Indecision

When one cannot rely on the rational input of the mind to make decisions, navigating life can seem like a daunting prospect. Indecision can result. The heart's guidance can also be misleading when emotional neediness is at the helm. When our inner child (and the rest of our inner family) are parented, the heart is fulfilled and becomes a reliable source of guidance. Decisions are based on the inner guidance of our inspiration.

+

3. Loss and Deprivation

Once cannot make a hole in the ocean. Loss must immediately be replaced by something else. The opening left by loss, like a tree felled in the forest, leaves room for something new to grow. By focusing on what is now possible, that was not before, we maximize the gifts of loss.

+

4. Victimization and Injustice

In feeling victimized, we lose our personal power by becoming an effect, rather than a cause. The environment is the expression of ourselves. Taking responsibility for it, and acknowledging that we change our environment by changing ourselves, is the way of the master.

=

Wanting life to change in beneficial ways, but losing sight of the fact that we accomplish this by changing ourselves is to abdicate the throne of self-determination.

The Pericardium and Circulation Meridian

1. Emotional Injury

The comfort for emotional injury lies in the self-sovereignty of inner balance. This is achieved by the contribution and expression of the sub-personalities: the inner child, inner nurturer, inner sage and inner warrior. The hard knocks of the world become bearable when we have a happy inner home.

+

2. Addiction

Addiction takes place when self-expression is suppressed or absent. It fills the gaps of self-abandonment until we come home to ourselves. In the rush of a life of duties, the dynamic balance of proactivity (action) and receptivity (rest) is often disturbed. The surrendered life rests during activity.

+

3. Jealousy

When we carry the burden of self-reflection, rather than self-examination, we create for ourselves the ball and chain of self-pity and self-importance. Self-examination ensures that we are living our highest truth. Self-reflection compares and contrasts ourself with others – the source of jealousy.

+

4. Regret

When we consider that the Infinite perfection of life unfolding underlies everything, we must also consider that there are no wrong choices or mistakes to regret. The choice to travel a road of shadow is to embrace the choice of hardship as our teacher, rather than inspiration. Both define the divinity that is in all beings.

=

To express authentically, from a purified heart, reveals the mystery of the self through our actions. Through unfolding self-knowledge comes self-love and self-regard. It is when we enjoy our own company that, being self-fulfilled, we find joy in interaction with others.

The Thyroid Meridian

1. Hopelessness

The complexity of life can cause feelings of overwhelm and hopelessness. The illusion of the many having more power than the one, is one of the most pervasive impediments to the self-empowerment of the individual. We have been standing in a hall of mirrors created by the matrices formed from our belief systems. If the hundreds of mirror images raise their hand when we do, how can they possibly have more power than the point of origin - the individual.

+

2. Depression

Depression is the unexpressed anger and frustration we feel, turned inwards. The frustration of not being able to make a difference is often at the root of depression. How large a difference we can make, is however, our choice. It all depends on how much responsibility we are prepared to take for our environment. We cannot change any part of the whole without affecting all the other parts.

+

3. Despair

The root of the feeling of despair is the desire to give up. The positive attitude of surrendering through trust in the perfection lying behind the appearances can become distorted into despair when we fail to raise our eyes above the storm. When we get drawn into the limited vision of man by engaging in their games, we become trapped in the mirrored world of despair.

+

4. Suicidal Tendencies

The desire to signal that help is needed through suicide attempts, is a desire to have someone else save us and validate our worth. The low self-esteem that precedes suicide attempts comes from deep feelings of self-abandonment. The world seems empty when our inner child, inner nurturer, inner sage and inner warrior are not whole and expressing. Creating a strategy to incorporate little things in our day that make our heart sing are stair steps out of such deep depression.

=

Finding at least one thing each day to be grateful for and one thing that makes us happy, breaks the pattern of despair and depression one step at a time. This signals the brain to release the hormones that establish well-being and thus our joyous response to life increases.

The Gallbladder Meridian

1. Rage

Within rage lie the elements of anger, frustration and desperation. It can be triggered by injustice, disrespect and other factors that block self-expression. It is a desire to break up that which imprisons and impedes. The method through which such blockages can be broken up to yield the energy and insights that they hold, is by finding what stagnant patterns they represent within us and letting those patterns go.

+

2. Impotence

Impotence can be felt when others or circumstances suppress our freedom of choice. But there is one choice that can never be taken away: the way we respond to what life delivers to our doorstep. We can choose to either feel victimized or to seek the gifts of insight it brings.

+

3. Self-importance

The self-importance we create for ourselves comes from a complete lack of perspective. Whichever standard of excellence is achieved is but part of today's dream within our eternal existence. The standard of today can be but the springboard for achievements of tomorrow, if we are humble enough.

+

4. Stagnation and Stuckness

Complacency born of the approval of others, or the comfort of our own prison bars of belief systems, is a thief that subtly steals our power. Stuckness comes when we are imprisoned by problems for which we can find no solutions. However, for every problem, the solution already lies within it. Think beyond the obvious and strategize your way out of the situation.

=

When we are ready to transcend an existing paradigm's boundaries, we often find ourselves feeling hemmed in and confined. The butterfly leaving the cocoon and the baby leaving the womb both feel the same discomfort that compels them forward, beyond present boundaries.

The Liver Meridian

1. Protectiveness

The need for protectiveness is the result of feeling that we live in an unsafe universe, ignoring the fact that we choose our reality by our attitudes – either haphazardly or masterfully. The protectiveness that we manifest in relationships comes from valuing laughter more than tears. In retrospect, we can see that tears have often been the greater teacher.

+

2. Desire to Save

The desire to save is the arrogant worldview that life manifests imperfectly and requires our assistance. If someone or something in our path need help, it is our privilege to assist because it is part of our next step. But many who feel unlovable, settle instead for feeling needed in order to boost their self-esteem.

3. Phobias

Phobias form because of misplaced terror. Terror that is nameless and huge is manageable when transferred onto something small and recognizable. Unless we find the insights of the original terror, continually repressing them creates a dialogue in the mind that clouds our perceptions and keeps us in ego-identification.

+

4. Obsessiveness
Obsessiveness results from believing firstly that we are overwhelmingly confronted with hostile forces and events that are unpredictable. Secondly, the notion that sustains obsessiveness exists because we think that we can control and contain it. Somehow the obsessiveness supports the illusion that we are able to make life more predicable. The quality of the journey is all we may contribute to through our chosen attitudes, but the acceptance of the unknowable, eternal journey of existence, allows us to relax and release the folly of attempted control.

=

To cultivate an eternal perspective, and a poetic point of view, sees life as an unfolding work of art. The knowledge that whatever choices we make from our highest truth, we are contributing in a unique way, releases the angst of inadequate performance on our part. Without fear of failure, we can approach life with aware appreciation.

The Outer and Inner Senses of Nature
The Key to Unlocking the High Heart

The high heart, located in the area of the sternum, is the additional turquoise chakra that the body uses within the reality of oneness. Eight chakras used in oneness, plus the seven chakras used in polarity form the fifteen-pointed star used by Rune Masters.

The resurrected life, beyond the opposites of the one and the many, can only be reached from a state of oneness because the turquoise, or eighth chakra, is the gateway out of duality. It opens by opening the gate between nature as an outer experience and nature as an inner state of being. It is recommended that the master study the profound truths revealed by the inner and the outer states of nature.

The 27 States of Nature – the Outer Experience

1. The interspecies interaction to awaken evolutionary possibilities
2. The delightful arena of diversity
3. Mutually stimulated interactive inspiration
4. The game of ingenious adaptability
5. Rich infrastructure of multi-perspectives
6. Interconnected awareness
7. The purification of experiences through the perspective of nonjudgmental innocence
8. Dissipating negativity through distributing the healing process through entrainment
9. The satisfying contentment of timelessness
10. Flawless cooperation with the rhythms of the heartbeats of eternity
11. The sexual tension of potential waiting to be birthed
12. Fertile possibilities through the exponential interaction of diverse life-forms
13. The resonant responsiveness to the emphases of man
14. Interconnectedness of the symphony of the many to the composition of the One
15. The energetic emanations into form, of the primordial substance of eternity
16. Endless variety of expressions from the original tones
17. Diverse conduits of eternal flow
18. Temporary capacitors of Infinite Intent
19. Articulation of the Eternal dance of grace

20. Diverse portals into eternal existence

21. The surrendered full expression of the diverse roles in the greater purpose

22. The pure and fresh interpretation of the breath of Source

23. The eternal current of love, fueled by the enjoyment of the adventure of self-discovery

24. Living from the still point of existence in formless form

25. The timeless arena for immediate responses to the magical perspective

26. The garden of discovery and play for the subpersonalities of man and gods

27. The effortless response of nature to the directiveness of innocence

The key to unlocking the mysteries of the cosmos is found in the response of nature as an inner state of being, to the never-ending pageantry of nature unfolding without.

The Equation of 27 External States of Nature

The clear, unselfconscious journey of the humble expression of majestic divinity.

The 27 Inner States of Nature

1. The pristine renewal of spring

2. The comfortable seasonal rhythms of activity and beingness

3. The resilient bending of the river reeds

4. The courageous shedding of the obsolete, like leaves of autumn

5. The ever-new perspective of the young on the oft-repeated migration of the birds

6. The unquestioning readiness for the next step of the baby bird's first flight

7. The unhurried journey of the wide river on its way to the ocean

8. The acceptance by the mountain stream of its transfiguration into a waterfall

9. The adventure of the dam's transcendence into a cloud

Eskaragot 49: Ekvravir-kirunet-manech

(From the Divinity Quest Divination card deck, available at alminewisdom.com)

10. Unstoppable flow of volcanic magma dissolving structured belief systems

11. Mysteries of uncharted potential whispered by the breeze to the aspen trees

12. The lighthearted tread of lifelike raindrops in the sand

13. The freedom of heartbeats: hooves of mustangs thundering across the plains

14. The wind the musician, the willow the harp, the song of the self plays from the heart

15. Courage through vulnerability, as the rabbit leads the fox away from her young

16. Yellow buttercups in vibrant hues, streak across the electric green grass. All life is a living work of art.

17. The swallows in thoughtless delight dart in graceful arcs through the sunset sky, graceful artistry through inevitable action.

18. The external observer, like the weather-carved mountain crags, watches as the ages roll by.

19. The movement of time, like the field of daffodils quaking in the intimate breath of the wind is an expression of infinite delight.

20. The howler monkeys, rustling the jungle canopy, shout their defiance at the approaching night: foolish the game of resisting life.

21. In the poise of surrender, the black swan sails serenely down the moonbeam's trail.

22. Having no destination, the downy cygnet feather drifts aimlessly on its adventure upon a gentle breeze.

23. In predictable white, the snowy barnyard gossips in hushed tones about the audacious indecency of the bold, red berries of the holly tree.

24. The hypnotic chorus of crickets in a starry night sings an adventure-weary grey cat to sleep on the back porch.

25. With sugary tones, golden finches chat in the blossoms of the orange tree. In the walled world of the garden, a child pauses at their exotic sound.

26. With one eye forward to see where he is going, and one eye backward to see where he has been, the chameleon makes his ponderous way along a branch.

27. Intricate lace on the wet sand, an edge of foam marks the fleeting accomplishment of the receding tide.

The Equation of 27 Inner States of Nature

The ever-unfolding mystery of the unknowable glory of the face of the Divine

The Final Equation of the High Heart

The clear, unselfconscious journey of the humble expression of majestic divinity

+

The ever-unfolding mystery of the unknowable glory of the face of the Divine

=

The miraculous transcendence of space and time through the joyous reunion of outer and inner space.

The Sigil of the Real High Heart

Provides Guidance for your Response to the Situation for Highest Outcome

The Sigil for the Life-Force Center of the Navel

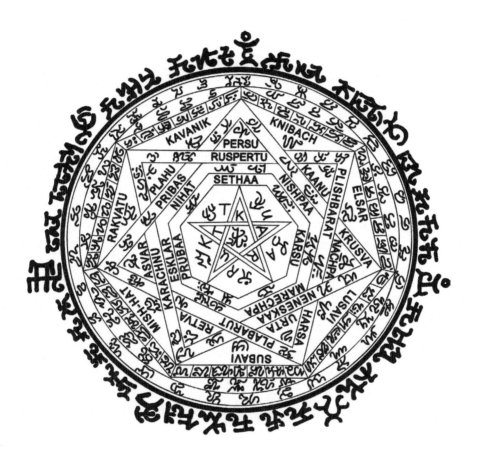

The Runes of
the Field of Mysticism

The Runes of the Field of Perception of Mysticism

The Runes of the White Rose

When a rune is drawn as a card or thrown as a stone and it faces right-side up, the attribute is present and dominant in the situation. Upside-down, it means that the attribute is lacking.

The Song of the Runes of Mysticism

The Song of Cooperative Surrender

1. The activation of endless possibilities through the alchemy produced by our unique participation with unfolding Infinite Intent.

2. Appreciative receptivity to the inspiration of the diversity of unfolding life.

3. The immaculate timing of automatic responses.

4. Trusting in the wonderment of benevolent life revealing itself.

5. Accessing the magic of the eternal moment through being fully present.

6. Enthusiastic participation in a masterfully performed dance of life.

7. An innovative response to unfolding existence through a unique perspective.

The 96 Runes of the White Rose

1.

The Proper Ratio
This rune represents the proper ratio between the Earth, the sun and the moon. Dynamic balance is present.

2.

Remove Belief Systems
Belief systems need to be discarded. When upside down, they are in the way of proper perception and are causing problems.

3.

Cooperation with the Divine Plan
The situation is for the enhancement of all life. Upside down means self-centeredness is present.

4.

Fertile Possibilities
The possibilities of the situation could lead to many opportunities. Upside down means potential possibilities are being overlooked.

5.

Cooperation and Partnership
Others and life's circumstances
will cooperate. If upside down,
expect opposition.

6.

Doorway of Transition
There is a decision ahead that
will change the direction of life.
There is no upside down position.

7.

The Opportune Moment
The time is right when the rune
is right side up. It is best to wait
when it is upside down.

8.

Indwelling Life
The situation should be dealt
with by altering the non-physical.
Upside down means the non-
physical reality does not support
the physical one.

9.

Beneficial Outcome
Expect success when this rune
appears right side up. It is best
not to proceed if it is not.

10.

Emotional Change
Emotions are changing below the
surface. If upside down, emotions
need to change.

11.

Trust
Trust is present in that the
situation is trustworthy or people
are trusting.

12.

Love
Love is present either in actuality
or in potential.

13.

Something is Overlooked
The correct answers come from
the correct questions. Look over
the situation again. If upside
down, a critical oversight has
been made.

14.

**Self-sovereignty through
Self-responsibility**
The core concept to living a
life of inclusiveness is to know
that your environment is your
expression. If you do not like it,
change what you express in your
life.

15.

Gratitude
It is time to increase something in
your life.

16.

Ghosts from the Past
Do not relive past patterns that no
longer serve. If upside down, you
are being drawn into something
that should be let go.

17.

Birth

Something new is conceived:
advantageous new beginnings.

18.

Assistance

Assistance should be given.
If upside down, assistance is
needed.

19.

Change of Destiny

Your destiny and the pattern
of life ahead of you is about to
change.

20.

Foreign Element

A foreign element is about to
enter the situation. This is like the
proverbial wild card.

21.

Creative Solutions
There is a creative solution that enhances all involved. When upside down, creativity is being stifled.

22.

Abundance
The situation will provide abundance in some form. If upside down, abundance will be withheld or reduced.

23.

Learning
Learning is taking place. The sooner lessons are learned, the sooner you can move on. When upside down, you are failing to learn.

24.

Guidance
Guidance is being given. When upside down, guidance is being ignored.

25.

Harmonious Interaction

Harmonious interaction is the result of either being of one heart or one mind, as in having a similar vision or goal. When the divergence between visions is too great, inharmonious interaction results.

26.

Change of Direction

Expect yourself or others to suddenly change directions. Take nothing at face value and be clear about what you feel.

27.

Levitation

A time of expansion and growth. Cosmic assistance for your endeavors can be expected.

28.

Hope

A possibility of success is strong enough for you to fix your eyes firmly on your goal and fan it with hope.

29. 　　30.

Loose Ends

You must not rest on your laurels even though things seem smooth on the surface. Multiple steps are required before the outcome is assured.

Incompletion

Right side up indicates good beginnings, but warns that many more steps are required to put the pattern in place and bring your desires to fruition. Upside down means that your initial steps are incorrect or will not bear fruit.

31. 　　32.

Humility

Do not take anything for granted. From our limited vantage point, we can know nothing. Even the smallest unforeseen contribution can turn the tide.

Waiting for the Future

Have patience while waiting for the next step to reveal itself. We do not go to the future, it comes to us.

33.

Parallel Scenario

Your interpretation of a situation is at total variance with the facts or the way another person views it. If upside down, be cautious – there are agendas.

34.

Return to Simplicity

Any situation can be reduced to one or two simple questions. Ask what it boils down to. Complexity is sometimes used by others to confuse you and hide true motives and agendas.

35.

Dynamic Geometry

Think out of the box, not allowing old belief systems to bind you to old behavioral patterns.

36.

Source

Perception is required to discern the eternal principle at work. You are in an archetypal situation in which you represent more than yourself.

37.

Luscious Possibilities
Serendipitous events await you. Awareness is key in seeing the endless possibilities before you.

38.

Challenge
Life has issued a challenge to see if you are worthy of the power it wishes to bestow. Let humility lead you on with impeccability as a shield. Approach the situation with courage.

39.

The Trickster
Goals can be achieved through play. Keep your sense of humor. Fluidity is essential.

40.

Influence
Act with utmost care. Vast ramifications hang on your every action. While considering others, it is crucial to do that which makes your heart sings.

41.

Inner Strength
Sometimes we have to go
through birth pains to reach a
higher level of existence. Let
inner strength and discipline see
you through the time ahead.

42.

The Unknown
Obsessing about questions drains
energy and lowers consciousness.
Face the unknown before you
with an empty mind and open
heart, avoiding the tendency to be
confused.

43.

Recognizing Sacredness
Recognize sacredness even in
obscure places. Look beyond
mundane appearances into
the foundation of perfection
underlying every soul and fueled
by Source.

44.

Imminent Explosion
Retreat and batten down the
hatches. Try to remedy the
situation, but be prepared for
confrontation.

45.

Flow
Time to hold on lightly to everything in your environment. Life is about to carry you into new possibilities. Trust the light of your mind and love in your heart to reach beneficial outcomes. Remain fluid.

46.

Self-government
Put your affairs in order and prepare for a growth spurt. Chaos can hold you back, so order in your environment, documents and relationships is required before the next step can manifest.

47.

Negative Pole
You are over-polarized into doingness, the proactive masculine pole. Bring more balance to your life by being more receptive. This is necessary to reveal what is or is not life-enhancing.

48.

Ancient Voices
What is about to occur comes from past existence. It is time for completion. You have evolved to higher levels, so let your heart be your guide. Baggage from the past must be let go.

49.

Seeing Behind Appearances
Use caution, things are not what they seem. Watch for signs to indicate reality behind the facade.

50.

Ascension
Situations can be turned into ascension stepping-stones through love, praise and gratitude. In the worst of circumstances, a glimmer of gratitude can loosen the ties that bind and set us free to ascend into higher consciousness.

51.

Authenticity
Listen to the voice of your heart to hear truth. Deep meaningful living takes place in the absence of social conditioning and labels. The rune urges restoration of authenticity in yourself or others. Truth is not being properly reflected. Upside down means there is deliberate untruth.

52.

Divine Assistance
Calling in multiple beings for divine assistance will be beneficial. Angels assist when we ask.

53.

Knowledge
More facts are needed before discernment can take place at the cognitive levels. Though the heart is the ultimate judge, the jury is still out – it doesn't have enough facts.

54.

Recovery
There will be gradual change for the better after hardship. Cooperate fully with changes that feel appropriate so positive results can manifest.

55.

White Magic
An opportunity to reveal the perfection of life is at hand.

56.

Closure
Time to close off that which no longer serves a purpose in your life. List all pros and cons and eliminate with grace that which does not enhance.

57.

Spiritual Gift
A spiritual gift will be found
in an unexpected place. Watch
carefully. Even the mundane can
produce abiding gifts of great
beauty.

58.

Shining Your Light
This is not the time to hang
back, but to step out of obscurity.
Time to be center stage whether
in leadership or in simply
expressing your gifts.

59.

Required Action
This indicates you are over-
polarized into inactivity and need
to counterbalance this by being
proactive. Over-polarization into
the feminine produces stagnation
and slows growth.

60.

Celebration
Find the high points in your
life and celebrate them. The
spirit of celebration gives
acknowledgement, increasing the
positive in our lives.

61.

Self-work
Time to uproot a specific flaw in your perception or to gain insights from experiences. When overdue, life unpleasantly forces us into introspection. Set time aside for self-work.

62.

Consideration
Yours or another's feelings need to be considered. The quality of the journey is as important as the goal.

63.

Exchanging Gifts
Everyone you meet in your day comes to give a gift and to receive one. The rune indicates this principle needs to be applied. Be generous with your praise and receive it openly.

64.

Removal of Limitations
Many fail to recognize new opportunities because they imagine old limitations to be in place. This is the time to take more risks than normally. Have faith in your ability to accomplish what previously seemed unobtainable.

65.

Speaking from the Heart
Time for you to voice your
feelings or to allow someone else
to do so, and then truly listen.
In this type of communication,
feelings should be valid
motivators in searching for new
solutions.

66.

Instinctual Nature
Known to some as 'wild woman'
or 'green man', is the inner
component to express. This subpersonality is the source of new
potential; allow it to come out of
the box.

67.

Ritual
Personal and family rituals can
create meaningful moments and
provide structure to family life.
Spiritual rituals create focus to
manifest intent. An opportunity
to incorporate ritual into your life
is before you.

68.

External Guidance
Be specific about a question you
want answered and then watch
for signs in your environment.
Trust what you see.

69.

Illumination
An influx of light is about to occur in your life. Take time to digest the insights that will be yours. It is a gift of grace that will bring changes for the better.

70.

Prosperity
A chance to prosper in a specific area of your life. When that window of opportunity opens, be prepared to put your labor and energy into it.

71.

Kindred Spirit
When kindred spirits meet, the effects ripple throughout Creation. The synergy of souls augments the effects of such interaction. A meeting with a kindred spirit is before you.

72.

Surprising Results
Right side up, the rune promises unforeseeable, but pleasant results. Flexibility is your best ally. Upside down, unforeseen results could be an unpleasant surprise.

73.

74.

Acknowledging Individuality
Knowledge of self or another is
needed in the specific situation
to which the rune applies.
Understanding our own and
other's strong and weak points is
very helpful in creating a proper
life strategy.

Mystical Experience
A mystical experience such as a
communication from the hidden
realms or the spirit world is
imminent. Take time for stillness
to allow it to happen and live
with heightened awareness.

75.

76.

Manifesting Potential
Previously unseen opportunities
are lurking around you as
potential. Pay attention to your
feelings, however irrational,
and observe signs in your
environment that indicate areas to
pursue.

Pretentiousness
Something is seen for more than
it is. It can also be the case that
though something is realistically
seen, its value to your life may be
overestimated.

77.

Change of Attitude
Your own or another's attitude
is blocking the way to creativity
and birth of the new. It must be
adjusted.

78.

Mastery
Mastery results from living in the
silence of the mind, but within
the full range of our emotions.
Do not permit yourself to be
pulled out of the deep strength
at the core of your being – your
connection to Source.

79.

Unfoldment
A portion of yourself or another
is not fully expressing. Nurture
all areas of your life into their
unfolding.

80.

Freedom
Time to break the shackles of
the value systems imposed by
others. Question the origin of
your motives and how strongly
seeking approval of others has
imprisoned your life.

81.

Raising the Kundalini

True strength and creative power arise when we are engaged in a love affair with life. This rune advocates sensuality through awareness as a way to promote the flow of energy.

82.

Mirror

The situation before you is a reflection of something you need to look at in your own life. To change the mirror, the change must begin within. We generally pull in mirrors of that which we are, have yet to develop or of what we think we have lost along the way.

83.

Fluid Support

When life supports us, it is often fluid, unexpected and not easily discerned. Fluid support indicates we have aligned ourselves with the Will of the Infinite and the Source of Power.

84.

Eliminate Protectiveness

In a cosmos where perfection underlies appearances, protectiveness is not a true cosmic frequency. The rune counsels you to replace protectiveness with trust.

85.

Accomplishment

That which has taken effort or toil is about to yield results. From now on, your efforts will pay off. Expect support in helping to birth the new.

86.

Dignity

An area of your life needs to be treated with more respect and dignity. It could simply be the acknowledgement of another's worth or the reverence for life.

87.

Different Approach

A change of strategy may be needed. The current flow of life may now be flowing in a different direction or your initial assessment must be rethought.

88.

Flowering of the Heart

A relationship is about to receive increased love and understanding to help it blossom. Recognizing everyday heroism in a friend can bring deeper respect and love.

89.

The Greater Cause
It is time to throw your support behind a greater cause. The rune could indicate that you must set aside individual differences and function from one heart and a common vision.

90.

Perception Changes
A series of swift perception changes could occur, meriting treating yourself and others with a great deal of flexibility. Life is in a state of flux around you; opposing the current would weaken your position.

91.

Trail Blazing
Do not seek outside advice, but be prepared to find yourself in a unique situation. Unexplored territory lies ahead. The signs in your environment can guide you through.

92.

Tribunal
Time for dues to be paid and justice done. Karma pertaining to this life is being called in. If upside down, expect injustice.

93.

The Messenger
A message of importance will be delivered. Sit in quietness with pen and paper in case it comes from the hidden realms. The message may also come through a sign in your environment. Be aware enough to see it.

94.

Augmentation
The small shall become large. Multiple contributions will bring fulfillment of a larger goal. By working on all aspects of your dream, it can come to full realization.

95.

Nurturing Into Fruition
Gentle coaxing is required to bring into full fruition that which is in its tender beginnings. Patience and gentleness coupled with perseverance will yield surprising results.

96.

Overestimation
It is unfair to expect behavior associated with levels of consciousness not actually possessed by another. Overestimating another simply because you do not like to look at flaws puts unfair pressure on them and sets you up for disappointment.

The Seven Steps of Mastery

Step 5

The Bridge of No Time

By combining the tones of the Pingala and Ida, the Master opens the gateweay to the inner and outer space of his being: The Bridge of No Time. It is here where he masters the unspoken communication of the Runes.

Almine

The Field of Perception of Metaphysics

The Wheel for the Runes of the Field of Perception of Metaphysics

Metaphysics studies the macrocosm in order to better understand the microcosm – individuated life.

Kesh asata vihek manasutvi

As below, so also above.

The metaphysical perspective examines the relationship of the one and the many. It studies the role of the one as an archetypal pivot point for all life.

The Song of the 70 Tones of Metaphysics
The Song of the Dance of Eternity

1. The greater vision of the never-ending journey.

2. The mastery of choosing realities.

3. The release of tension through choosing the eternal perspective.

4. Personal power through fluidity.

5. Visions of awe-inspiring grandeur.

6. The dynamic balance of spiritual maturity.

7. Speed of accomplishment through timelessness.

8. The deeper vision of expansive perspective.

9. Knowing the self through the cosmic laboratory.

10. The dissolving of judgment through timeless vision.

11. Elevated perception by withdrawing from games of manipulation.

12. Beyond existing paradigms.

13. Freedom from mortal boundaries.

14. The boundless vision quest.

15. The flight of the heartsong.

16. Grandeur of fields of hope.

17. Expressed microcosmic splendor.

18. Parting the curtains of the holographic universe.

19. Affecting the fractal design.

20. Observing the extent of personal power.

21. Unending inspiration.

22. Participating in unfolding splendor.

23. Co-created journey.

24. Ascending the throne of self-responsibility.

25. Singing the song of the grand adventure.

26. Understanding endless discoveries.

27. Aware exploration of the unobvious.

28. Complete trust in the subtle knowing of the purified heart.

29. The effortless choices of the inspired journey.

30. The gratification of masterful manifestations.

31. The gift of increasing clarity.

32. The quest for revelations of the face of the Infinite.

33. Complete confidence through humility.

34. The contented acknowledgment of the unknowability of life.

35. The never-ending deepening of the meaning of life.

36. The awakening of heartfelt praise for the unfathomability of life.

37. Self-regeneration through the enquiring mind.

38. Perpetual alchemy through enthusiastic participation.

39. Revealing the perfection through uncluttering the mind.

40. Gratitude and praise, inspired by observing the miraculous.

41. Living in the presence of holy communion with the Infinite.

42. Effortless manifestations of Infinite Intent.

43. Creative responses to the challenges of life.

44. Choosing from the boundless perspective.

45. The reverence of walking on holy ground.

46. Self-acknowledged sacredness.

47. Becoming the pivotal origin of your environment.

48. Living in the stillness of the eternal moment.

49. Creating new accessibility to potential by reaching beyond the horizon.

50. Turning heavy responsibilities into a mountain-climbing adventure.

51. The recognition of opposition as the shadows that define the artistry.

52. Seeing the familiar in an unfamiliar way.

53. Opening the intimacy of an inclusive heart.

54. Opening the bounteous gifts of life through aware appreciation.

55. The magical results of an impersonal life.

56. Unrestrained enthusiasm for embracing the mystery.

57. Participating in the totality of life as an artistic expression.

58. The rapture of the poetic perspective.

59. Hearing the enticing whispering of the magical journey.

60. The joyous journey of excellence in expression.

61. Viewing limitation as a temporary guidance system.

62. Uncovering the miraculous unfolding of self-individuation.

63. Replacing experiential wisdom with the discovery of new possibilities.

64. The illuminated flight of high mastery.

65. The activated responses of the inner senses as the impetus for action.

66. Holy allies on a sacred journey.

67. Opening gates of trust by expressing love, praise and gratitude.

68. Expressing inner states of nature in resonance with outer manifestations of nature.

69. Infinite possibilities through awakening magical expectations.

70. The lighthearted traveller on the river of luminosity.

The Sigil for the Song of the Dance of Eternity

The Alchemical Relationship between the Infinite and the Individual

The Star of the 70 Tones of Metaphysics – Karash-asteve

The Star of the 70 Angel gods – Estnaviritva

The numbers on the inner star represent the 70 Angel gods.
The outer numbers represent the 70 Tones of Metaphysics.
(See the keys on the following pages.)

The Outer Star: The Names of the Tones

1.

Lisperu

2.

Nensraklu

3.

Virasesvu

4.

Abrahut

5.

Sku-ater

6.

Nespara

7.

Kivasut

8.

Aruklana

9.

Bitresut

10.

Ararat

11.

Melskor

12.

Avruta

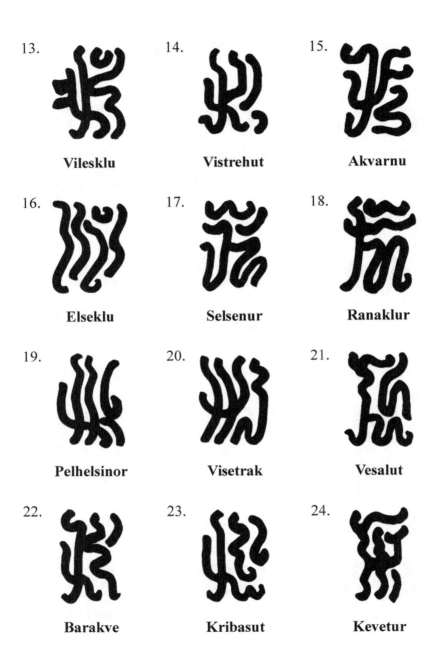

13. Vilesklu

14. Vistrehut

15. Akvarnu

16. Elseklu

17. Selsenur

18. Ranaklur

19. Pelhelsinor

20. Visetrak

21. Vesalut

22. Barakve

23. Kribasut

24. Kevetur

25.

Lesutvit

26.

Keresunu

27.

Selesanu

28.

Karasu

29.

Menetur

30.

Vrisbaru

31.

Eksparu

32.

Pliseta

33.

Turesut

34.

Kivinar

35.

Klesatar

36.

Ninesklar

37.

Ruktavahek

38.

Trusetar

39.

Bisalaruk

40.

Ekbravik

41.

Belesunur

42.

Efrenasur

43.

Sumereta

44.

Kevehut

45.

Tabasus

46.

Melisklar

47.

Visanuk

48.

Parabuk

49.

Araspletar

50.

Efrevesve

51.

Kiranatuk

52.

Briterena

53.

Skuharana

54.

Keseruspaha

55.

Mekenur

56.

Sisalhur

57.

Raspaklit

58.

Mevrenanus

59.

Bisheletut

60.

Avramanus

61. 
Krisatura

62. 
Ekvrehus

63. 
Skelstare

64. 
Vranamus

65. 
Puharstanu

66. 
Histavrenu

67. 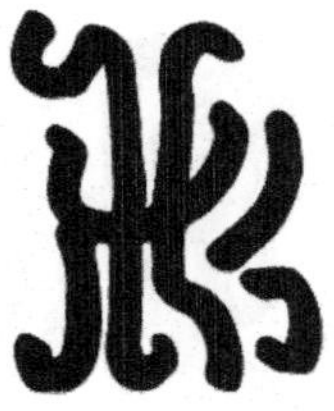
Visebelesu

68. 
Arskaklatu

69. 
Vresparatut

70. 
Menesasablut

The Inner Star: The Names of the Angel gods of the 70 Tones of Metaphysics

Note: The 96 Angel god names are associated with the Runes. The 70 Angel god names are associated with the Principles of Metaphysics.

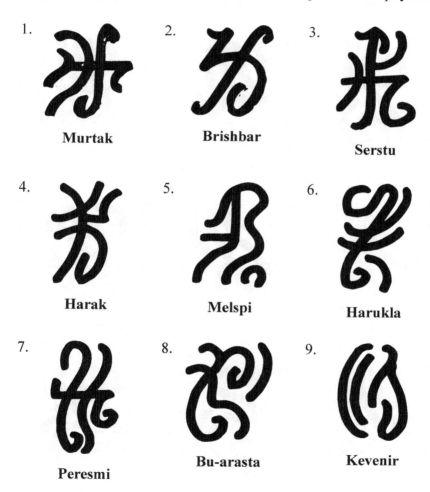

1. **Murtak**

2. **Brishbar**

3. **Serstu**

4. **Harak**

5. **Melspi**

6. **Harukla**

7. **Peresmi**

8. **Bu-arasta**

9. **Kevenir**

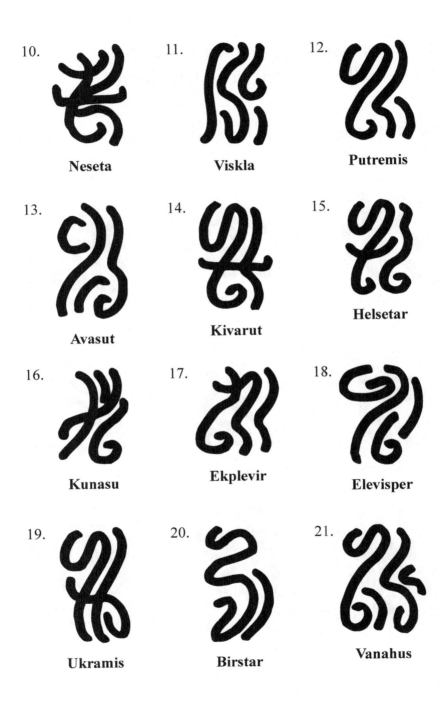

10. Neseta

11. Viskla

12. Putremis

13. Avasut

14. Kivarut

15. Helsetar

16. Kunasu

17. Ekplevir

18. Elevisper

19. Ukramis

20. Birstar

21. Vanahus

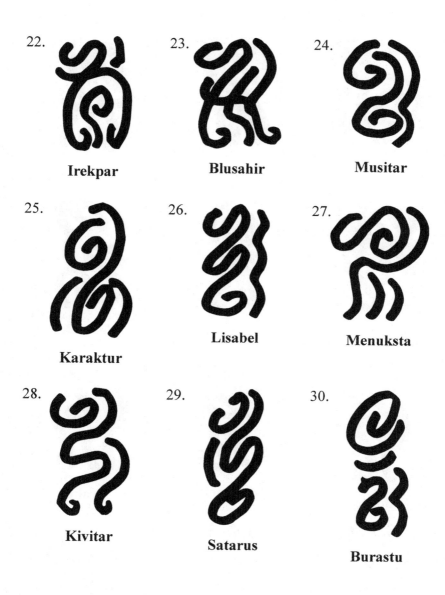

22. **Irekpar**

23. **Blusahir**

24. **Musitar**

25. **Karaktur**

26. **Lisabel**

27. **Menuksta**

28. **Kivitar**

29. **Satarus**

30. **Burastu**

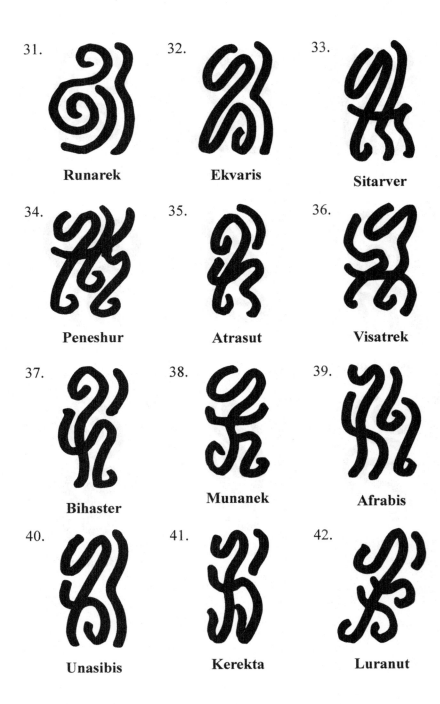

31. Runarek

32. Ekvaris

33. Sitarver

34. Peneshur

35. Atrasut

36. Visatrek

37. Bihaster

38. Munanek

39. Afrabis

40. Unasibis

41. Kerekta

42. Luranut

43.
Ninahes

44.
Kepreta

45.
Ukvrasut

46.
Esenet

47.
Alakpa

48.
Bivarusata

49.
Enesekve

50.
Tabaru

51.
Puhakles

52.
Spiraknu

53.
Estraminus

54.
Kalsapur

55.

Arumanus

56.

Bristal

57.

Peletrusena

58.

Keskelet

59.

Kapurnaha

60.

Sisatur

61.

Viraberesva

62.

Kunastur

63.

Blirehekva

64.

Erasnanu

65.

Harsnanu

66.

Kiratar

67.

Lusananu

68.

Vrubekle

69.

Akparus

70.

Helsenuk

Preparing for Resurrection
A Ceremony to Combine the Ida and Pingala

Introduction

This ceremony combines the Ida and Pingala, which coordinates and integrates the function of inner and outer space. This is the goal of the Grand Master of the Runes, and the blessing of the sixth field of the Perception of Godhood.

Its symbol is the white owl with a 15-pointed star. A white owl is the symbol for death. In this case it is the death of the old through Resurrection. The cooperation of the inner (symbolized by the number 8) and the outer realities (symbolized by the number 7) to produce fluid form thus becomes number 15. Fifteen is the symbol for inner manifestation.

Creating the Ceremonial Space

The Inner Ring

Create a ring of *12 stacks* around the area where you will be lying for the ceremony. You may lie on the floor, a massage table or a bed inside this ceremonial circle of 12 stacks.

Place the first stack at the point above where your head will be located. Each stack contains 2 **Big Wheels** with the highest number wheel on bottom and the lowest number wheel on top.

The Outer Ring

Create a 2nd ring of *13 stacks* outside of the first ring using 2 **Small Wheels** in each stack. Each stack has 2 Small Wheels with the highest number wheel on bottom and the lowest number wheel on top.

Creating the Bottom Stack

The bottom stack is to be placed directly under the navel area. All wheels and sigils may be laminated.

- Stack the **Power Wheels** (also called the **Grand Master Wheels**) in the following order: first number 3, then 2 and number 1 on top.
- On top of the previous stacks of wheels, add from ***The Wheels of 65 Wisdoms* numbers *1, 2 and 3*** with number 3 on bottom and number 1 on top.
- Next place on the stack the ***Sigil for Establishing a Life of Formless Form.***
- On top of that place the ***Four Equations of the Keepers of the Bridge of No Time.***
- On top of that place ***the Alchemical Equation of the Power Wheels 1, 2 and 3.***
- Lastly, place the ***Combined Alchemical Equation of the Power Wheels.***

Creating the Top Stack

The components are given in the order they should be stacked. Place the stack face down on the navel of the Grand Master.

- ***The Androgynous Equation of the 65 Angel gods of the Bridge of No Time***
- ***The 65 Feminine Equations of the Angel gods of the Bridge of No Time***
- ***The 65 Masculine Equations of the Angel gods of the Bridge of No Time***
- ***The Power Wheel of the Resurrection***

Preparation for the Ceremony

- The music titled ***The Bridge of No Time*** should be ready to play during the ceremony.

- Have a list of the *96 Runes of the Field of Perception of Godhood* and their meanings handy near the place where you will be positioned during the ceremony.

Performing the Ceremony

- You are lying in the center of the ceremonial space created by the stacks of the 12 Big Wheels (inner ring) and the 13 Small Wheels (outer ring).
- Place the bottom stack under your back, directly behind the navel area.
- Place the top stack with images towards the body over the navel area.
- Begin playing the music of *The Bridge of No Time* (or the Hadji-ka Brainwave Meditation). Hold the list of the *Runes of Godhood* in your hand.

Method

1. Relax by deep breathing. Continue until a deep meditative state is reached.
2. Imagine sinking through the navel area into the space known as the Haaraknit, which means 'place of no time'. It is the meeting place of inner and outer space.
3. Envision a private lake and beach with black water shimmering in the moonlight. This water purifies everything that it touches.
4. Lying on the soft beach or in the shimmering black water, look at the runes in your hand and call them into the black lake, reading and comprehending their meanings.
5. Imagine each rune being pulled in through the navel area, entering the lake's water and moving through the bottom of the lake into inner space.

6. As each rune is understood and moved through the navel area, feel the subtle, rippling response within.

7. The more often this ceremony is repeated over the course of a few weeks, the more the 10th row of DNA will become functional, and the more inner guidance will be heard.

8. Close with the words:

Mishata Uravich Huresbi
The mystery reveals itself to me.

The 24 Big Wheels

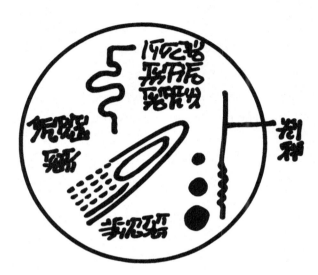

Big Wheel 1

Big Wheel 2

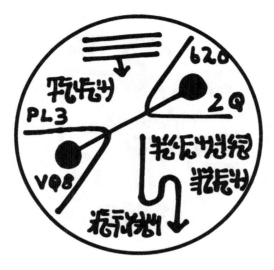

Big Wheel 3

Big Wheel 4

Big Wheel 5

Big Wheel 6

Big Wheel 7

Big Wheel 8

Big Wheel 9

Big Wheel 10

Big Wheel 11

Big Wheel 12

Big Wheel 13

Big Wheel 14

356

Big Wheel 15

Big Wheel 16

Big Wheel 17

Big Wheel 18

Big Wheel 19

Big Wheel 20

Big Wheel 21

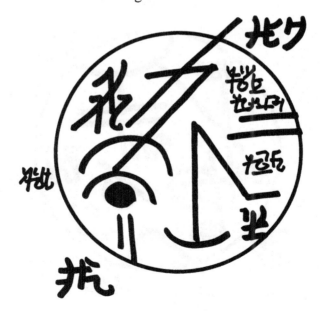

Big Wheel 22

Big Wheel 23

Big Wheel 24

The 26 Small Wheels

Small Wheel 1

Small Wheel 2

Small Wheel 3

Small Wheel 4

Small Wheel 5

Small Wheel 6

Small Wheel 7

Small Wheel 8

Small Wheel 9

Small Wheel 10

Small Wheel 11

Small Wheel 12

Small Wheel 13

Small Wheel 14

Small Wheel 15

Small Wheel 16

Small Wheel 17

Small Wheel 18

Small Wheel 19

Small Wheel 20

Small Wheel 21

Small Wheel 22

Small Wheel 23

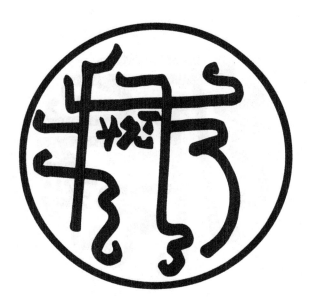

Small Wheel 24

Small Wheel 25

Small Wheel 26

Grand Master Power Wheel 1

Grand Master Power Wheel 2

Grand Master Power Wheel 3

The Wheels of 65 Wisdoms

Wheel 1

The Wheels of 65 Wisdoms

Wheel 2

The Wheels of 65 Wisdoms

Wheel 3

The Sigil for Establishing a
Life of Formless Form

Equations of the Keepers of the Bridge of No Time

I

Nikrit-avrana

+

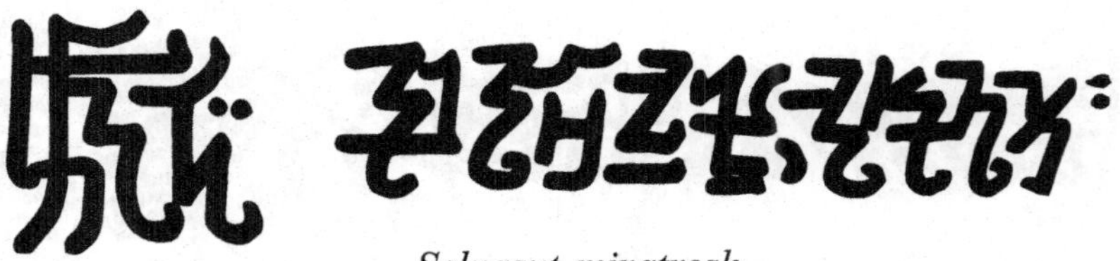

Selvasut-miratresh

=

Elsekla-subetvi

Equations of the Keepers of the Bridge of No Time

2

Kitrehat-selevi

+

Mistratve-sersanek

=

Uchbek-mishtranik

Equations of the Keepers of
the Bridge of No Time

3

Iset-elevreni

+

Kasur-sebahik

=

Mestu-uhunisavich

Equations of the Keepers of
the Bridge of No Time

4

Kiratret-suhatvi

+

Achklavit-savahech

=

Mistar-esunavet

The Alchemical Equation of Power Wheels 1, 2 and 3

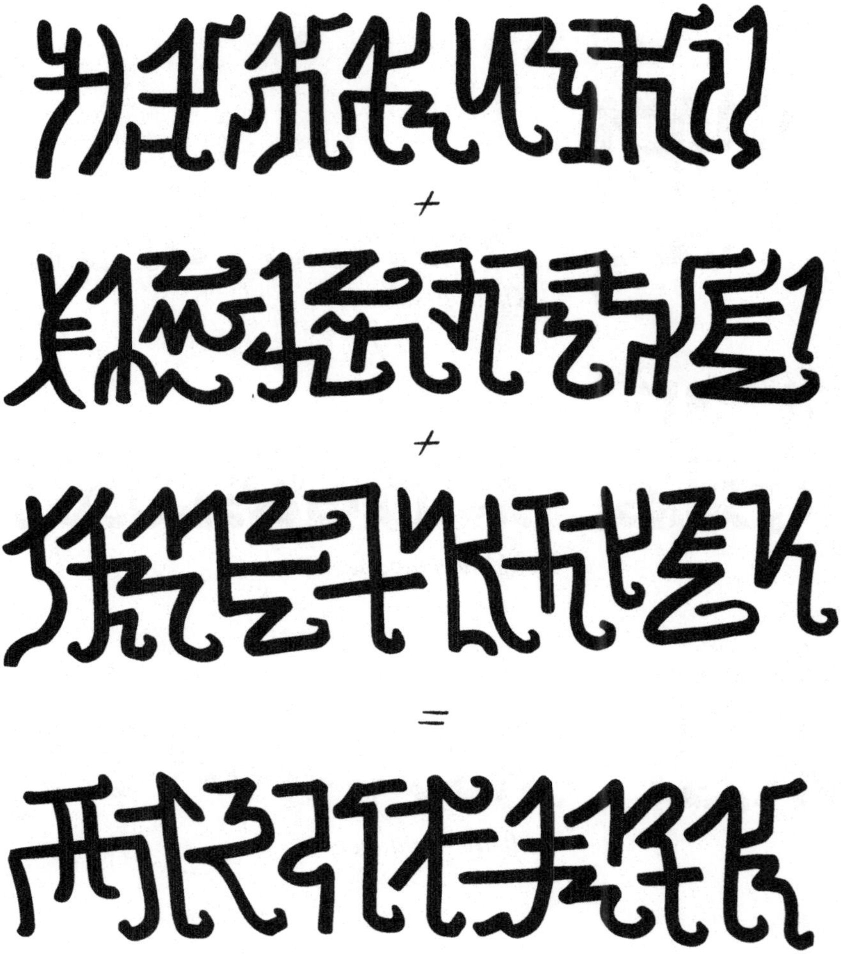

+

+

=

The Combined Alchemical Equation of the Power Wheels

Androgynous Equation of the Angel gods of the Bridge of No Time

Dissolving the tyranny of linearity

+

Fashioning individuated being through emphases

=

Living in the Haaraknit's freedom

Feminine Equations of the 65 Angel Gods of the Bridge Into No Time

1. *Pelekvirista* – Trust in benevolence +

2. *Tru-a-usutrane* – Surrender +

3. *Kaarnesh-istuvaa* – Peace from an eternal perspective +

4. *Estravirista* – Acknowledging unfolding perfection +

5. *Ku-uhurit-estavu* – Release of all vantage points +

6. *Estalvi-usurut* – Childlike wonderment +

7. *Karish-ersalvu* – Enchanting journey +

8. *Klubarsat-huruvat* – Unfolding delight +

9. *Nishkelarnu* – Complete release of tension +

10. *Rutsalarut-kilspa* – Anticipated fulfillment +

11. *Karusnunesta* – Dissolving expectation +

12. *Arakhursva* – Cherished living +

13. *Fruvabach-esalvi* – Dissolving relationships +

14. *Pahunasabi* – Dissolving all programs +

15. *Kaarikhelsava* – Knowing purity +

16. *Kinichsta-blaheshvavi* – A life of no opposites +

17. *Ustre-ninuhas* – Unconditional Oneness +

18. *Bruha-vachbri-nenusta* – Secure mastery through Oneness +

19. *Ku-uhalesh-stavabi* – Contented adventure +

20. *Michspa-nanunesh* – Lightness of being +

21. *Urustra-nenish* – Clear knowing +

22. *Virspa-vilshvravek* – Exalted living +

23. *Pruhusata-aklatvi* – Boundless abundance +

24. *Niselnut-arsta* – Impeccable interpretation of Divine will +

25. *Kilservat* – Refined enjoyment +

26. *Archba-esterva* – Enhanced quality of life +

27. *Nusatpahur-nanunit* – Indivisible beingness +

28. *Giriknit-hasvi* – Fluid stability +

29. *Uskut-blavabaa* – Authentic expression +

30. *Kuhurut-etravit* – All-knowing humility +

31. *Arak-pahar-salavi* – Effortless genius +

32. *Aruna-sahetba-ur* – Endless inspiration +

33. *Usutranet-kalsat* – Self-trust through surrender +

34. *Arch-baruk* – Conduit of grace +

35. *Bilsabi-arsta* – Delighted surprises +

36. *Vrubet-ararak* – Complete carefreeness +

37. *Karusut-pleba* – Appreciating life +

38. *Vravu-esta-plahe* – Delighted aloneness +

39. *Rutpa-ninusut* – Dissolving the illusion of discordance +

40. *Arusat-klavespi* – Finding home in the Oneness +

41. *Arak-bravista* – Complete acceptance of life +

42. *Nuset-araspravaa* – Dissolving family ties +

43. *Esek-valabi* – Dissolving the need to understand +

44. *Nustra-harahich* – Unrestrained enthusiasm +

45. *Plubes-arstavaa* – Enjoyment of the physical +

46. *Vrubik-harsta* – Unsentimental appreciation +

47. *Nespa-kelhatrut* – Dissolving all evaluation +

48. *Atravaa-mishat* – Emphasis through appreciation +

49. *Uset-blavuk-harsta* – Beginningless existence +

50. *Isat-nanustru* – Never-ending innovation +

51. *Kirit-archva* – Trusting exploration +

52. *Vrabis-eselha* – Releasing all knowledge +

53. *Prahut-arstava* – Dissolving desires +

54. *Krubet-aravespi* – Embracing the paradox +

55. *Urchvaa-hiretvi* – Acknowledging life's newness +

56. *Karus-esta-varavit* – Releasing all linear time +

57. *Kiliset-asbi* – Finding life's humor +

58. *Minish-elesut-bravi* – Excellence of living +

59. *Krunaspriha* – Releasing through graceful change +

60. *Arut-aleshkla* – The levity of the plan +

61. *Vilisat-blu-ablak* – Freedom through Oneness +

62. *Brive-miselnu* – Dispelling the tyranny of form +

63. *Arnaklatve* – Affecting life only through the real +

64. *Vrunabilesva* – Luscious rejuvenation of form +

65. *Archnut-hesba* – Entering the gate of no-time =

Karnak-virisba-eklet-nanusa
The Purity of Absolute Oneness

Masculine Equations of the 65 Angel Gods of the Bridge Into No Time

1. *Karasut-uvabi* – Revealing the underlying perfection +

2. *Isita-plahuvabi* – Recognition of intrinsic value +

3. *Kenuch-baharaspi* – Freedom from social conditioning +

4. *Keresvileshvavi* – Self-discovery through removing illusion +

5. *Uhurunesvi-eklesva* – Unimagined discoveries +

6. *Ustrubaravespi* – Magical encounters +

7. *Isitaa-manuch* – Increased resources through release +

8. *Uselviminish-hastra* – Channeled resources +

9. *Bishet-echkelesvi* – Dissolving the need for war +

10. *Aklas-baras-vravi* – An end to inertia +

11. *Erestravi-eklasvu* – Inexhaustible supply +

12. *Nunesprahusplavi* – Self-purification +

13. *Manash-harastu* – Self-sustenance +

14. *Plavabi-erehesvi* – Growth through grace +

15. *Barachva-nunesvi* – Changing the ordinary into the extraordinary +

16. *Pihistaravu-nesvi* – Exponential increase +

17. *Paarachvu-stereblu* – Leverage into a more joyous unfoldment of life +

18. *Nanasvi-elesva* – Production of magical surprises +

19. *Istrechvi-minash* – Enjoyment of transcending boundaries +

20. *Hustelvi-iklech* – Unexpected rewards +

21. *Baaresminestra* – Glory expressed through equations +

22. *Berechstavatu* – Cooperative manifestation +

23. *Mishet-harastu* – Offered blessings +

24. *Varashuhavetvi* – Self-regeneration +

25. *Misetnunasetvavi* – Actualizing potential +

26. *Spiharut-varanesvi* – Creation of new realities +

27. *Sahabatruha-nesva-velesvi* – Recognition of Infinite potential +

28. *Kerchbaranustrahit* – Exponential elevation of consciousness +

29. *Selvamisertu* – Limitless expression, the Song of the One Life flows through me +

30. *Ninesvilespelevra* – Ever-expressing wholeness +

31. *Ustech-heresva* – Limitless supply of resources +

32. *Vires-estavu-viblat* – Experiencing self as all that is, as the One Life +

33. *Harchba-sihes-usteva* – Full appreciation of the exquisiteness of the One Life +

34. *Uselvi-iskleva* – Fluidly surrendered expression of Infinite Creation +

35. *Harstava-isklevu* – Acknowledging ourselves as the unknowable +

36. *Karasut-skelvavi* – Effortlessly regulated self-regeneration +

37. *Nusetpeleshut* – Awareness of the depth of existence +

38. *Isitrebishvabet* – Expanding our ability to appreciate Infinite resources into expression +

39. *Suhit-elesklavrabit* – Acknowledging the contentment of being Home +

40. *Uruch-misvastra* – Honoring the holiness of our being as the expression of Infinite's depth +

41. *Nuvalasblik-stereva* – Graceful acceptance of our own greatness as the One Life +

42. *Asbrahut-selvevat* – Entering into the incorruptible purity of the One Life +

43. *Krubahach-ustreva* – Embodying excellence in expression +

44. *Virs-esklahut* – Empowerment through acknowledging Infinite expression through our being +

45. *Bruvavek-birechstu* – Pivoting life into newness +

46. *Nistrahutblavek* – Willing cooperation with the Divine +

47. *Eresutmistrave* – Self-sustenance through being a sluice for Infinite resources +

48. *Kluvavech-huvabit* – Delightful surprises through changeless change +

49. *Niselvu-asarat* – Universal recognition of excellence +

50. *Kuruhit-plave* – Releasing all definitions +

51. *Erchbaranit-kelesta* – Self-sustaining sovereignty +

52. *Varanis-preheva-unis* – Beautiful beingness +

53. *Arachmiravetvavi* – Abundant expression as the One +

54. *Karutpleheva* – Spontaneous authenticity of living +

55. *Kirasatpiretplevavu* – Complete release of self-reflection +

56. *Kelesetvi-nusavi* – Living beyond matrices through self-regeneration +

57. *Kusataa-berechsata* – Individuation through Infinite Beingness +

58. *Kelsaprahesvravi* – Living beyond all previous standards of excellence +

59. *Arasach-birespravi* – Dissolving boundaries through limitless Beingness +

60. *Mirasachvelushvi* – Fluid incorruptibility through surrender +

61. *Miseret-travu-belestra* – Exquisite luminosity in expression +

62. *Karavitmiseru* – Conduit of unfolding Oneness +

63. *Estra-bivarus-trava* – Embracing seeming contradiction +

64. *Kerenech-setrabit* – Virtuosity within the One Life +

65. *Kluhus-ustra-barus* – Seeing the perfection behind the
imperfection =

Perevahitvu-peleshnasat
The coming home into joyful Oneness

The Power Wheel of Resurrection

The Ida and Pingala

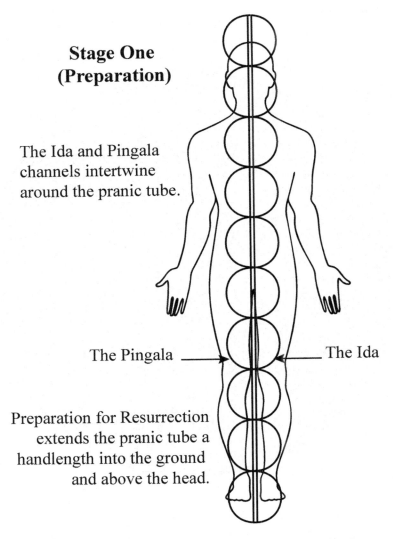

**Stage One
(Preparation)**

The Ida and Pingala
channels intertwine
around the pranic tube.

The Pingala ——————→   ←—————— The Ida

Preparation for Resurrection
extends the pranic tube a
handlength into the ground
and above the head.

It is highly recommended that the master practice the three
levels of the *Sacred Breaths of Arasatma* to obtain the full use
of the pranic tube.

The Runes of the
Field of Metaphysics

The Runes of the Field of Perception of Metaphysics

The Blue Light Runes

When the seven fields of perception shall unite
Then shall emerge the runes of blue light
Seven sets of runes – these are the fifth
Shall in alchemy combine and to a power object give birth

In hypnotic trance does humanity dwell
Mind-controlled and under a spell
Three books of holy writings shall arise
To free humanity and clear their minds

Books are they, yet not as they seem
As power objects must they be seen
Vast alchemical equations, with powers unseen
They dissolve the hostile enslavements that all may be free

Amongst humanity gods have come
Through self-government, to uplift everyone
Their perspective is as vast as eternity
But mind control, like hypnosis, contracts their perspective into
egocentricity

Subtly it comes, as entertainment disguised
The programs to enslave and blind man's eyes
Controlling suggestions, while deeply he sleeps
That enter his mind from seven perceptional fields[7]

---

[7] The assemblage point is a ball of light about the size of a fist, located an arm's length behind the heart and a little bit to the right. It determines our band of awareness, which reality we access. A slight movement of the assemblage point puts us in an altered state, such as meditation.

The Book of Runes subliminal information dispels
Black magic is undone by the Book of Spells
Implanted behavioral control from aliens received
The Book of Star Transmissions[8] will set you free

These three books are sacred tools
Their power will remove shadows from you
Keep them near you, until a bond forms
Until an impervious field, like a holy space is born

Then shall you your authenticity maintain
When programs are removed, pristineness remains
Your home shall again be sanctified
That in holiness you there may reside

[8] See forthcoming book – *The Star Races Speak.*

The 96 Concepts of the Runes of the Field of Perception of Metaphysics

The Runes of the Blue Light

The concepts of the fifth set of runes all pertain to dissolving the limitations of the matrix: the illusion of being imprisoned by the appearances of time and space. Study these concepts well before using the runes. They will guide you by stimulating inner capacities to see beyond the obvious, and will indicate trends of which direction life is unfolding into.

Carried with you as a power object, they emphasize certain aspects of potential carried within the moment. This strengthens certain parts within you, and like an alchemical equation, facilitates certain outcomes. They are therefore also devices to help achieve positive manifestations.

The 96 Runes of the Blue Light

1.

Subtle Nuances
Unwavering trust in your inner senses.

2.

Monitoring Inner Responses
Sensitive awareness to subtle currents of feeling in response to life.

3.

Inspired Guidance
Following the guidance of what evokes inspiration within you.

4.

Illuminated Insights
Searching for inspired illuminations on the journey through aware appreciation.

5.

Graceful Release
Graceful release as the doorway
to higher possibilities.

6.

Impeccable Timing
Impeccable timing through
courageous action.

7.

Masterful Response
Skillful discernment in
responding to opposition.

8.

Uplifting Focus
Choosing your reality through
emphases.

9.

Releasing the Unacceptable
Respecting yourself as the source
of your circumstances.

10.

Enhancing Life's Quality
Masterful orchestration of the
quality of your life through
chosen attitudes.

11.

Remembered Timelessness
Moving through the illusion of
opposition through surrendered
allowing.

12.

Bold Expression
Living boldly in the knowledge
that a risk is simply something
mind cannot control.

13.

Thinking Outside the Box
Seeking excellence that can only
be found beyond the confines of
the known.

14.

Unconditional Authenticity
Unconditional faithfulness to
authenticity.

15.

Intuitive Solutions
Feeling the solution that lies in
an inseparable union within the
problem.

16.

Trusting Self-guidance
Clarity through trusting intuitive
knowing.

17.

Power through Cooperation
Mastery through cooperation
with the moving forces of Infinite
Intent.

18.

Renewed Vitality
Cooperation with the self-
renewing forces of the cosmos
through releasing resistance to
life.

19.

Empowerment through Trust
Power as an inseparable way of
living in cooperative trust.

20.

Abundant Expectations
Graceful transitions as a steady
supply of resources.

21.

Profound Shifts
Dramatic shifts as a surge of
power needed for momentum for
large accomplishments.

22.

Deeper Understanding
Empowered actions through
broadened perspectives and
deeper understanding.

23.

Releasing Limiting Beliefs
Being an explorer of
consciousness beyond self-made
boundaries.

24.

Embracing the Unknown
Building moral courage by
embracing the unfamiliar.

25.

Childlike Enthusiasm
Lighthearted dancing with the
unknowable by releasing the
need to know.

26.

Co-creating Reality
Self-selected realities through
emphases.

27.

**Reverence through
Acknowledged Divinity**
Uncompromising vision held of a
luminous reality of godhood.

28.

Rapid Fruition
Knowing the gap between cause
and effect to be a fluid option.

29.

Creating Self-change
Fully expressing in the moment
that which you wish to become.

30.

Magnificent Breakthroughs
Expressing the unique song of
the self in all its splendor.

31.

Contented Journey
Moving effortlessly through the
illusion of density.

32.

Maintaining Poise
Serenity within the storm.

33.

Expanded Influence
Embracing the storm within the
serenity.

34.

Radiating Presence
Dispelling despair through
radiating presence.

35.

Anticipating Clear Answers
Choosing a state of anticipated
clarity over confusion.

36.

Guiding Signs
Adept interpretation of the
symbolic language of the dream.[9]

---

[9] See the free *Dream Dictionary* at www.spiritualjourneys.com.

37.

Expanding Enquiries
Pioneer of passionate exploration.

38.

Empathic Connection
Communicating with the
aliveness of all things through
respect.

39.

Cutting Binding Ties
Releasing the need to be
understood by acknowledging the
unknowable nature of life.

40.

Making Pivotal Choices
The courage to live a self-
determined extraordinary life.

41.

Meeting the Challenges
The poise of a master's self-
confidence in responding to
circumstances with ease.

42.

Following Inner Knowing
The grace of automatic action at
one with unfolding life.

43.

Blessings through Challenge
Releasing the challenge to bring
creativity to the dance of eternal
life.

44.

Supported Vision
Trusting life to support
boundlessness in action.

45.

Boundless Living
Contributing to the evolution
of life through pushing the
boundaries of originality and
excellence.

46.

Passionate Action
Uninhibited passion articulated
into action.

47.

Contributing Originality
Vibrant originality in inspired
expression.

48.

**Impeccability of Highest
Choice**
Unwavering integrity through
living the fluidly unfolding
highest truth of the moment.

49.

Magical Synchronicities
Sensitive attunement to the beckoning call of the magical life.

50.

Hidden Insights
Inquiring curiosity to follow the never-ending mystery of existence.

51.

Careful Communications
Impeccable and inspired speech through heightened awareness.

52.

Increase through Gratitude
The reverent stewardship of personal resources. The increase of strong suits through grateful acknowledgment.

53.

Stand Your Ground
Courageous willingness to stand
alone if integrity requires it.

54.

Uncluttered Vision
The dedicated commitment to
absolute clarity.

55.

Unselfconscious Response
Authentic expression as the
highest truth.

56.

Removing Judgment
The metamorphosis of life
through the release of judgment.

57.

Focused Vision
The compression of time through the contracted focus.

58.

Subtle Information
The fullness of an interdimensional life.

59.

Releasing Emotional Neediness
The emotional self-sovereignty of the life that is self-referring for approval.

60.

Seeing the Larger Vision
The engaged observer of the artistry of life in expression.

61.

Lighthearted Approach
The lighthearted steps of no regrets.

62.

Grounded Practical Wisdom
Deep abiding kinship with the Earth.

63.

Sensitivity as to Consequences
At-oneness with the natural world and its communication.

64.

Structured Flow
The dynamic balance of disciplined spontaneity.

65.

Acknowledging Diverse Contributions
The complete acceptance of diverse levels of consciousness.

66.

Sacred Rhythms
Embracing the sacred rituals of interaction and solitude.

67.

Taking Self-responsibility
The empowering perception of the environment as an expression of the self.

68.

Validating Inner Knowing
Mature interaction with beings from other dimensions.

69.

Confident Creativity
The confident acceptance of
being the architect of your reality.

70.

Inner Growth
Building a rich and multifaceted
inner reality through silent
solitude.

71.

Beneficial Influence
Flooding your outer experiences
with inner peace and
contentment.

72.

Emotional Self-sovereignty
Transcending the need for
acceptance and conformity.

73.

Excellence in Action
Refusing to compromise by
accepting mediocre living.

74.

Embracing the Adventure
Choosing the wonderment of the
cutting edge over stagnation.

75.

Self-inspiration
Rejecting complacency by
becoming your own source of
inspiration.

76.

Guidance of the Heart
Being true to yourself even if it
disappoints others.

77.

Honest Assessment
The fearless exploration of light
and shadow.

78.

Finding New Strengths
Allowing adversity to stimulate
greatness.

79.

Lighthearted Journey
The lightness of a burdenless past
by knowing the presents rebirths
the past.

80.

Fluidity
Fluid and adept maneuvering
around the dysfunctional
behavior of others.

81.

Releasing Programmed Responses
The diligent eradication of the programs of the mind.

82.

Humble Approach
Refusing to enslave yourself by not building a personal matrix through belief systems.

83.

Ignoring the Trivia
Allowing the unpleasant experiences of life to move through you, unhindered by resistance.

84.

Changing Perspectives
The moment reveals its potential to the eyes of the poet, or the awareness of the sage.

85.

Grateful Acknowledgment
To fight for what we want limits receptivity. To acknowledge what we have, increases it.

86.

Empathic Compassion
With compassion, see the negative emotions of others for what they are: the cry of one who believes themselves to be an abandoned, fleeting expression of life.

87.

Release Comparisons
Do not envy others, for they are trapped in their reality of duality in which excess in one area, creates shortages in others.

88.

Beware of Uniformity
Do not identify with any group, lest their dharma becomes yours to resolve – a high price to pay for the illusion of belonging.

89.

Self-sovereign Effortless Knowing
Become impervious to subtle controlling influences that are undetected, by refusing to be influenced by the opinions of others.

90.

Openness To Receive
Do not feel indebted in the face of generosity. It is yourself giving to yourself.

91.

Self-examination Required
In ruthless honesty with yourself, know the origins of your actions – whether they stem from mastery or neediness.

92.

Acknowledged Innocence
To indulge illusion and limited perceptions in yourself is to invite karma to brutally erase the shadows that they cast.

93.

Fuller Self-expression
Unsung songs of the heart cannot be denied. Find ways to express them so that addictions may not arise.

94.

Committed Learning
Extract insights from the experiences of others and yourself, so that life can evolve beyond them, rather than having to repeat them in repetitive cycles.

95.

Silent Leadership
Determine to live the exhilarating life of one who lives far beyond the multitudes. This is the highest service you can render.

96.

Chosen Attitudes
Choosing to live in a reality shaped by attitudes and choices derived from the highest truth, where the view is the breathtaking vistas of eternity.

The Seven Steps of Mastery

Step 6

Constructing The Bridge of No Space – The Bridge between the Unknowable and the Unknown

The heart travels blithely where the mind does not dare to go. For the heart still remembers what the mind cannot know.

~ Almine

The Field of Perception of Godhood

The Wheel for the Runes of the Field of Perception of Godhood

Terech sahu pele-usvi nanuhach
Awaken now the divinity within

The perspective of Godhood knows the Source of its inspiration to be the Infinite Intent speaking through the response of the 672 inner senses.

The God Merkaba and the Twenty-Six Concepts of Mastery

1. Human sexual hormones carry programs of attraction that can override reason or even attachments of the heart. Anything designed to affect another's behavior against their better judgment is defined as black magic. Hormonal control is therefore a black magic program designed to protect the survival of the species.

2. Those who were created in the god kingdom but who walk among men in forgetfulness have far less human hormones in some circumstances. Hormone replacement therapy seems necessary after a certain age. The attraction factor can be achieved without indiscriminate enforcement by mastering the rotation of the fields around the body.

3. In a god being who is awakening to their expression of godhood through the process of resurrection, the fields around the body elongate. These fields are referred to as the merkabic fields or merkaba.

4. Life at a lower level, such as the human level, has three star tetrahedrons around the body. These are the shape of three-dimensional Stars of David, each having two interlocking, three-sided pyramids. The three star tetrahedrons occupy the same space around the body: one spinning to the left, one stationary and one spinning to the right.

5. The points of these three star tetrahedrons reach a hand length above the head (for the top pyramid) and a hand length in to the ground beneath the feet (in the case of the bottom pyramid, called the earth pyramid).

6. In the case of a highly evolved being, the two interlocking pyramids are no longer equilateral (having equal sides), but are elongated to about a hand length plus approximately 10 inches (22 cm). Envision this change occurring in the star tetrahedrons around your body.

7. To create a tool of these fields that can regulate receptivity (attraction towards something) or proactivity (propulsion directed outward): the three star tetrahedrons must have their sun pyramids at the top, spinning separately from the earth pyramids at the bottom. In the case of the human star tetrahedrons, this will create a sphere of light. The elongated star tetrahedrons of god beings will create a luminous egg-shaped field when spun this way.

447

The Merkaba of the Human Level of Evolution

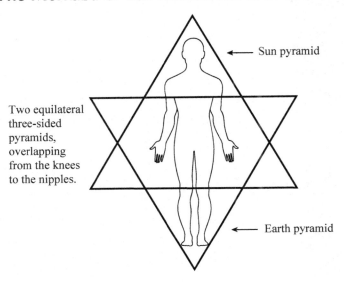

Sun pyramid

Two equilateral
three-sided
pyramids,
overlapping
from the knees
to the nipples.

Earth pyramid

The Merkaba of the God Level of Evolution

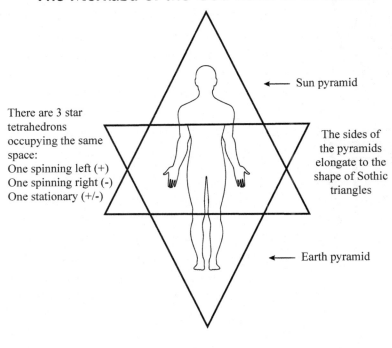

Sun pyramid

There are 3 star
tetrahedrons
occupying the same
space:
One spinning left (+)
One spinning right (-)
One stationary (+/-)

The sides of
the pyramids
elongate to the
shape of Sothic
triangles

Earth pyramid

Merkaba: Separating and Spinning the Star Tetrahedrons using Breaths

Directions

- Draw in a deep breath and force it out, silently commanding the sun pyramid of the left-spinning star tetrahedron to spin left at the speed of light.
- Draw in a deep breath and force it out, commanding the sun pyramid of the stationary star tetrahedron to spin left at the speed of light.
- Draw in a deep breath and force it out, commanding the sun pyramid of the right-spinning star tetrahedron to spin left at the speed of light.
- Draw in a deep breath and force it out, commanding the left-spinning earth pyramid to spin right at the speed of light.
- Draw in a deep breath and force it out, commanding the stationary earth pyramid to spin right at the speed of light.
- Draw in a deep breath and force it out, commanding the right-spinning earth pyramid to spin right at the speed of light.
- Repeat breaths 1-6, commanding that the spinning of the tetrahedrons go beyond the speed of light.

Luminous Egg formed from Spinning the Merkaba

The top is spinning left, or counter-clockwise

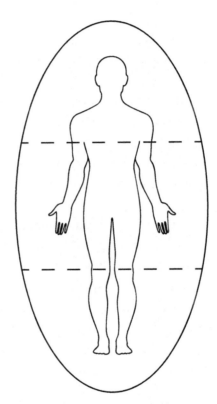

The top and bottom though spinning in different directions overlap in the middle.

The bottom is spinning right, or clockwise.

Luminous Egg formed from the Spinning Bodies of Man

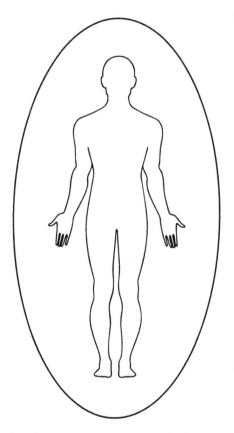

The luminous egg, or cocoon, is stationary.

8. The god being lives from a level of life that transcends individuation formed by clustering the building blocks (sub-atomic particles) of life. The luminous cocoon of a human consists of the seven bodies of man formed from sub-atomic particles. The god being forms his luminous egg, or cocoon, from the non-atomic matter that exists beyond the duality of the mirrored world.

9. The god being's cocoon is a dynamo of resources and creates autonomy. The human gets his resources from the law of compensation: the back and forth movement between two poles. But this energy requires more energy to produce than it actually generates. Eventually man's energy runs out, resulting in aging and death.

10. The energy the god being generates is directed through a created field of hope, (the more accurate term for energy in non-atomic matter is: impetus of intent). This creates a second energy source that can be called a perpetual alchemical combustion. Through this the god being becomes a cosmic energy generator.

11. With extended vision a god being can be seen to have a blue ball of light behind the navel. When the god being cooperates with the voice of Infinite Intent that ripples as inspiration through the 672 subtle inner senses, alchemical combustion takes place. The blue ball ignites into a blue-white little sun that creates a luminous field around itself.

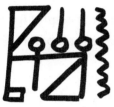

12. The field generated by the god beings blue-white little sun can be made smaller or larger depending on its purpose, and what the god being wants to energize. It can be duplicated and placed over certain areas to sustain, heal or to raise consciousness. It can be generated by using the breath.

Generating the Little Sun and its Field with Breath

Directions
- Place yourself in a meditative state.
- Start to see the blue ball (about the size of a grapefruit) behind the navel.
- Direct your attention to a specific area or topic. Feel what you are inspired to do.
- See how your inspiration ignites the ball and with each outbreath, allow it to grow larger and larger.
- On the third or fourth outbreath, force the breath out and let it explode into a field – the little sun will be formed.

- The little sun can be transferred to another location or kept around the body; it will be a dome that will completely enclose the luminous cocoon.

13. Non-atomic matter is extremely responsive to intent, and the one who wishes to master wielding it must become very sensitive to inner and outer senses' responses to inner inspiration and outer stimulation. Breath is used to destructure the obsolete and to create a new form or reality in its place. It is helpful to do the Merkaba spinning exercise right before doing this exercise.

Destructuring Illusion with Breath

14. Structure is held in the gap between the breaths. Form becomes fluid like the waves of the ocean, to effortlessly fall away when we eliminate the gaps. Release of birth and early childhood trauma occurs with repeated use of this exercise.

15. Breathe in and out in a comfortable rhythm that eliminates the gaps between the breaths but does not result in hyperventilation. Be aware that strong emotions may flush up as a result of this exercise.

    - Envision what you want to dissolve, and see it slowly disintegrating.
    - Continue this for at least ten minutes, preferably for twenty minutes.

Creating a Field of Manifestation

 16. Start to spin the top half of the Merkaba around your body faster than the lower half. Instruct it to spin faster at the following ratio: 7 to 3. The masculine will spin seven times for every three times that the feminine spins. The force of your breath is used to accelerate the spinning.

 17. With the forced out breaths, expand the blue-white ball behind the navel until it explodes into a field of blue-white light and reappears as a glowing sphere in the area of the navel.

 • Move this field and sphere to the area where you wish to manifest something new, carefully listening to Infinite Intent through the stirrings of inspiration within.

 18. With long out breaths, breathe it into existence. Envision the shape of what you want to see forming in your reality from the atomless, primal element, like a cloud in the sky or a wave appearing on the surface of the ocean.

 • Continue until you have a detailed image forming. Allow your heart to rejoice over it as though it is already in your reality.
 • See the blue-white energy source feed it energy (the impetus of your intent), until it is a firm reality in your life.

The God Merkaba and Hormones

19. When a particular part of the Merkaba is spinning faster because of your command, the increased speed only lasts about 30 to 32 hours. Normally the two halves of the Merkabic egg spin at the same speed, unless particularly instructed to speed up. This will affect the masculine or feminine expression of your body and takes the place of survival-based hormonal programs as you live in an existence of primal, matterless matter. It must therefore be used judiciously or it could cause an imbalance (women may get facial hair growth, for example) with prolonged use.

20. When desiring to receive something such as abundance from your creation of new aspects of your reality, spinning the masculine half faster to create it, and then alternating it with the increased speed of the feminine, receptive half of the Merkabic egg should be done.

    • Allow the proactive top half to spin for approximately 30 hours and then command the two halves to spin at equal speed (use the forced breaths).
    • Only then do you command the feminine, right-spinning lower half of the Merkabic egg to spin faster. The ratio should again be 7 to 3.

21. When the proactive part of the luminous egg, or cocoon, is being sped up, it must be done with a specific purpose. Envision what you want to accomplish as you speed it up. The exception is in the case of a 'hormonal' imbalance, where more masculine energy is needed. When increasing the feminine, or receptive for reasons other than to balance the feminine energies in the body, a filter should be created as to what you are open to receive. As you increase the feminine rotational speed, state clearly that you are open to for example: support, abundance, new opportunities and resources, etc.

22. The balance between self-determination, freedom of choice and surrendered trust has always been a mystery to lightseekers. However, they are two sides of the coin of energy management: Opposing life leaks energy. Not contributing our unique perspective to life, our greatest gift to the One expressing as the many fails to generate energy. It is therefore a draining attitude to be solely passive in the face of unfolding existence, rather than to understand the revealed insights and to embrace them as our own.

The Gift of the Blue Ball of Godhood

23. The blue ball of godhood located behind the navel is ignited by becoming one with Infinite Intent. It then becomes a blue-white sun of self-determined size. It can be a meter (about 3 feet) in diameter, or large enough to enclose the luminous cocoon around a god being (the oval formed by the god Merkaba). This can be sent to enlighten and protect as many people or places as you like. It will always reform around the body.

24. When this blue-white sun is enlarged around the body (use deep inbreaths to blow it up with intent, like blowing up a balloon), a change takes place in the body: every cell becomes an incorruptible, blue-white little sun. You have become an additional energy source for the Earth and her creatures. Every cell has become an additional energy source for you.

The Gateway of the High Heart

25. Only from oneness can the reality of atomic elements be left behind. The reason is that in oneness, the gateway out of duality and its mirrors becomes accessible. In polarity, seven main chakras are used. In oneness, the reality of the cosmic dream, eight are used. The turquoise chakra of the high heart becomes active. Native tribes in the northern United States have traditionally worn turquoise on their sternums. The teachings that have endured through the ages, say it is where earth (green of the heart) and sky (blue of the throat chakra) meet. It is also the place where inner and outer space meet.

26. The figure eight of the cosmic journey through the four directions has kept life going around and around the disc of life (the figure eight is merely a twisted loop, or ring). To leave this two-dimensional, rotational journey, inner and outer space must be combined. To do this, one part of the loop has to flip over, forming a Mobius strip. The unique construction of a Mobius strip joins inner and outer space as one. The high heart is the place where this life-changing blending of inner and outer occurs, where life and death become one through resurrection. The event happens by combining inner states of nature with outer states of nature.

459

The 96 Riddles of The Bridge of No Space – The Bridge Between the Unknown and the Unknowable

1. Eternity pulses in a grain of sand.

2. From a pure heart the river of eternal possibilities flows.

3. The cycles of expressed life as the rise and fall of the Infinite's eternal breaths.

4. The night breeze whispers its unfathomable mysteries to the garden of the moon.

5. The treasured discovery of the beginning of the golden thread that leads into the labyrinth of the unknowable.

6. Timeless revelations broadcast through rings of time.

7. With the innocent majesty and the comfortable greatness of a velvet cloak, the Goddess takes her place upon the throne.

8. The frog chorus draws the curtain of mystery, revealing the strange beauty of the kingdom of the moon.

9. Like a spring in the desert, the fountain of living waters from the Goddess flow forth.

10. Oceans of stars swirl along the veils of the dancer, gliding in fluid grace with every move.

11. In a shimmering stream, stars pour forth from the silver bowl of the moon.

12. Subliminal choruses of unsung songs, wait for the Goddess to rise with the moon.

13. Unexpected teachings from the trickster entice the weary traveler into the magical land.

14. Luminous yellow fragrance couched from unfurling petals by the pink notes of dawn.

15. A sapphire blue puddle cradled in the mighty tree, reveals the depth of the eternal sky.

16. Aglow, the temple gates reveal themselves as dusk deepens and the first star shines.

17. Mists in luminous tonal swirls dance the dancer. Crystal encrusted taffeta folds shape the song.

18. The music of the wind writes itself as it traces my unfolding, eternal face and shapes my endlessly forming form.

19. A butterfly flutters through the windows of the night, while whisperings of fallen stars move through eons of forgotten time.

20. A turtle releases snow-white eggs into the cradle of the sand, while the moon looks over the abyss of the night.

21. True love it was, when I felt her scent peacefully penetrating my being as in a magical spell. Dancing the dance of the dream, we instantly travelled to unseen worlds.

22. The Ida and Pingala, like sentinels they stand, guarding the way to the sacred temple where silence meets the dawn, and the moon garden sings its song on fragrant notes.

23. On a joyful breeze, over the field of peace, the little blue moonchild rides on the back of a dragonfly nestled between her wings.

24. The nightingale rolls his silver notes like beads across the black dome of the sky. The great dragon stirs from his slumber.

25. The yellow Asian chrysanthemum unfolds its petals in the shifting shades of dawn, in the afterglow of a silver moon.

26. In pregnant anticipation, the Earth's belly expanded as she awaits the rebirth of the Children of the Dragon.

27. The bridge of no space, like the bridge of moonlight across the ocean is there, yet it is not. It is to be felt and not said.

28. A single dewdrop on the edge of a silken leaf, reflecting the faces of the ages.

29. A pair of children's feet in the rich black soil, mapping out the path of joy.

30. In Nature She rests, white and still, like marble waiting. Soft rainbow flowers stretching endlessly, caress Her mystery.

31. Soft golden light: the Mothers' gift the angels bring to water in shimmering streams, the thirsty eyes of humanity.

32. Bring glad tidings to the weary, leave the fear behind. Magic is alive and well, the Goddess walks the land.

33. Unicorns follow Her gentle luminous presence as she moves across the fields. Where she steps, field flowers grow.

34. On a rainbow bridge I walk across the soft blue sky. Intentions manifest effortlessly from my hands.

35. In the mist, the lady bug flies, guided by feelings of never-ending color.

36. The heartbeats of the universe, like the wing beats of the dove, beckons us to dance to its rhythm, the interpretive dance.

37. The Goddess spreads the veil of fertility across the starry skies. From the delight of her dance sunds are born and moons bask in her luminous glow.

38. Each life-form, a portal into the unknowable. Just follow the path of mystery through the heart of the rose.

39. In a vehicle of blue-white light, upon a bed of roses, sail upon the ocean of mystery onto the shore of wisdom.

40. In the ancient libraries of the marrow of the bones, the deep knowing of the magic life is stored. Custodians of the holy are we.

41. The unprogrammed life of pure expression enters through the doors of the temple of the hallowed journey that never ends.

42. Like two swans matched in flight, one white and one black, the eternal grace of the dance of courtship between the masculine and the feminine takes place.

43. Leaves lift the wind and the flowers bring the spring – in the domain of the eternal Queen.

44. Like a sea of faces, crowds cover the land. Through eternal eyes, grass dancers in the wind.

45. The breadth of the land through the eyes of the eagle – with an eternal perspective, She navigates the way.

46. Like soap bubbles adrift on the wind, planetary systems float through the ages and then are gone.

47. A water –fey follows the moonlit silver bridge across the ocean and beyond.

48. The moonlight on the snow reveals a treasure trove of thousands of diamonds, pristine and untouchable.

49. The moose pauses in a snowclad field, watching the silent symphony of the Northern lights.

50. Fireflies, like little lamps in the moss, light the way for a forest stream. It is a night of courtship for the fairies.

51. Inspired by the light of a full moon, the owlet pushes his head through the cracking eggshell. The frog chorus grows still in awe at such a poetic wonder.

52. In an impossible song, the suns and planets sing to one another of ages gone by, and the gossip brought by traveling comets.

53. Carrying the sky upon his back, the caterpillar commands the army of his many feet. The golden finch laughs at such comedy.

54. In an opulent display, the snail travels on a road of silver in and elegant spiral coach.

55. The deep roots of the tree listen to the entertaining stories of the children of man held in the libraries of the soil.

56. In the lavender-blue night, among sparkling stars, unicorns cavort and play, running with golden hooves across the Milky Way.

57. When life is seen with the eyes of a child, time stands still before such purity.

58. To become the contradiction of being all or nothing is to bathe in the ocean of infinity and to flow like a current of life under the silver moon.

59. Illusion is the Eternal Artist's tool that paints a landscape of light and shadow, where the rays of the sun reach like fingers through the veils of mist.

60. The wisdom of the Goddess is not to label or explain, but to listen with rapture to the mysterious music of an unseen flute that leads us through the forest of untold secrets.

61. From the depth of the water, the magical kingdoms call. Unknown treasures are waiting to be received. When the Goddess awakens, the gift is ready.

62. Split the void and ride on butterfly wings. To become the contradiction is to become what we have always been: unknowable.

63. Awaken forgotten dreams that slumber like black pearls of great
    worth in the heart of the oyster.

64. Travel on the back of a black swan down the rainbow river into
    the self. Find there the pristine existence.

65. Hear the fragrant notes in the silence between the notes. It is there
    where windows into eternity are kept.

66. Time becomes timeless when the spiral of the opened heart spirals through. Then the true home is revealed behind the appearances.

67. Like a fragrant wind, the presence of the Divine Feminine carries the fertile seeds of great expectations.

68. Like the warm touch of silken skin, the inner senses envelope us in soft folds of eternal romance.

69. Through the alchemy of inner and outer senses, the orgasmic explosion pushes life into unchartered territory.

70. With the courage of a six-legged lion, and inner vision lit by moon rays, fall into the depth of your being.

71. Emit the fragrant song that carries the codes of a new dawn upon the wind, with lightheartedness let it begin.

72. While the Goddess slept, her dreams were caught. Under the rainbow of the moon shall they awaken.

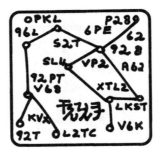

73. In self-confident flowering the lily disregards the fences made by man.

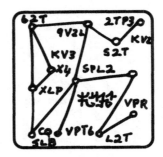

74. With the regenerative power of the phoenix, the mysterious and unexplainable presence of the Goddess births itself from the death of the old.

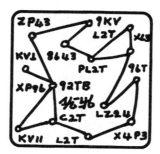

75. Crowned by moonbeams, adorned by the stars, wild woman
    dances to the song of her heart and the symphony of the night.

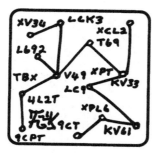

76. Let the Hearts of the Dragons melt in devotion to the tones
    of purity in the Mother's voice. Then shall the Earth walk the
    rainbow bridge.

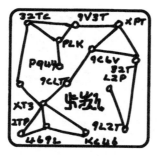

77. In the darkest night, let the blue moon within light the way and
    the dark sun shine upon your path.

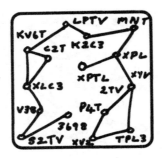

78. The eternal full moon of the opened heart and the starlit sky of the Haaraknit to guide and clear the way.

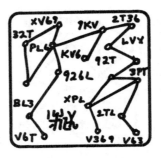

79. The high alchemy of the blue moon and the black sun in their fertile union.

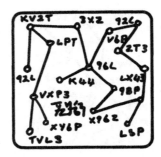

80. Living in the eternal poetry of being a flowering energy source of the cosmos.

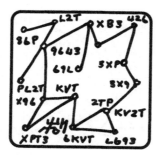

81. Skywalkers like beacons of hope for humans, shall be at ease in the resurrected life of both worlds.

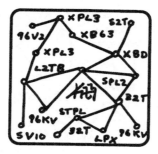

82. God beings among man, interpretive dancers on the stage of existence.

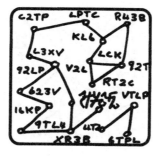

83. Remembering that the kingdoms of the moon and sun never have been separate, the healing dew of divinity waters all life.

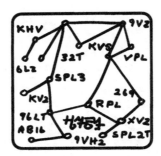

84. The secrets of elements of not time and space are held in the sand
    dunes of time since before subatomic intelligence obscured the truth.

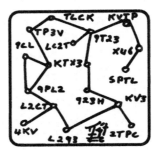

85. Those who have walked the bridge of no time and no space
    become bridges between the finite and the Infinite.

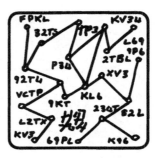

86. In the beauty of eternity, upon an endless road of discovery, it is
    but an expression of myself I see. All I can ever do is find me.

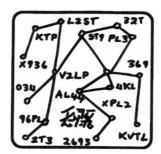

87. Black light shines as brightly to the inner eyes that see. Black and white light never have separate been.

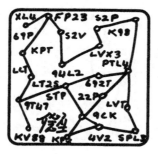

88. Within the white light's heart, the black light lies unseen. Only to be awakened in the light of the dream.

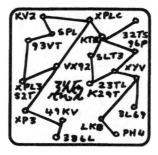

89. Choose in which reality you wish to walk and be, through emphases this choice is made by a resurrected being. Alternate as you will, these realities are theatrical stages of your choice.

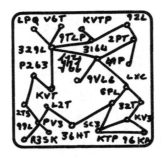

90. Realities are the miraculous responses of unclustered matter.

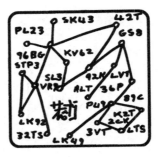

91. Heightened sensitivity as the required state of being to become the master artist of unarticulated matter.

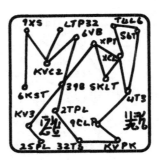

92. Living a miraculous life of genius beyond false humility that abdicated effortless knowing for recycled knowledge.

93. The evolved luminous cocoon as a tool of manipulating the expression of receptivity and proactivity.

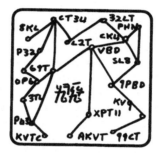

94. Through ever-renewed expression, like the formlessly forming clouds, the mysteries of deep revelations are revealed.

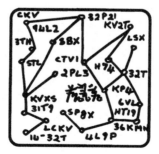

95. Replacing binding, mummified memories of the past with ever new, reshaped knowledge.

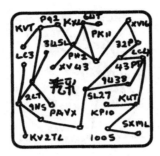

96. Manifesting the fluid tapestry of the environment through the rotational speed of the evolved luminous cocoon.

The Runes of the Field of Godhood

The Runes of the Field of Perception of Godhood

The Runes of Godhood

To live from the field of perception of godhood is to access the unifying force that sustains and animates all life forms. Living godhood implies living from an open-hearted intimacy that touches and ignites the core of divinity: the spark of the Infinite in all life forms.

To live from the authentic core of our being is to allow the current of Source to direct our actions and to align us with the power of Infinite Intent. Through the contribution of our unique perspective combined with Infinite Intent, a high alchemy takes place that forms and evolve our reality; our unique experience of the expression of Source.

The 96 Runes of the Lion's Gate

1.

Claiming Your Sovereignty

2.

A Higher Purpose

3.

Masterful Interpretation

4.

Subtle Currents of Communication

5.

Compassion through Objectivity

6.

Humble Acceptance of Learning Opportunities

7.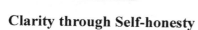

Clarity through Self-honesty

8.

The Restoration of Balance

9.

**Simultaneous Receptivity and
Proactivity**

10.

Reconciled Opposites

11.

Creative Contribution

12.

Synergistic Cooperation

13.

Activated Potential

14.

Unexpected Impetus

15.

Re-established Fluidity

16.

Optional Reality

17.

Self-determinative Quality of Life

18.

Timeless Perspective

19.

Greater Outcome

20.

Comfort with not Knowing

21.

Watching for Signs

22.

Rise Above the Situation

23.

Unforeseen Contribution

24.

Masterful Inner Change

25.

Elevating Emotions

26.

Watching for Inspiration

27.

Graceful Lessons

28.

New Possibilities

29.

Magical Results

30.

Strongly Affecting Others

31.

Attention to Details

32.

Seeing Beyond Existing Boundaries

33.

Achieving Your Own Support

34.

Observe from Different Angles

35.

Harness Your Supply

36.

Go Beyond Your Comfort Zone

37.

Clarity through Humility

38.

Retain Your Originality

39.

Releasing Judgment

40.

Self-acknowledgment

41.

Live As Though It Is Forever

42.

Excellence Beyond Expectation

43.

Moving Beyond Opposition

44.

Pay Attention to Feelings

45.

Courageous Adventure

46.

Take Time for the Inner Life

47.

Intuitive Knowing

48.

Consider the Effects

49.

Appreciative Acceptance

50.

Reveal Your Feelings

51.

Release Future Concerns

52.

Immaculate Timing

53.

Agendaless Cooperation

54.

Embrace Humanity

55.

Exploring Options

56.

Getting to Know Deep Enjoyment

57.

Trust Your Intuition

58.

Release Old Beliefs

59.

Embrace Multidimensional Guidance

60.

Fluidly Changing Roles

61.

Acknowledge Unknowability

62.

Optimistic Attitude

63.

Enjoy the Process

64.

Be True to Yourself

65.

Engaging in New Experiences

66.

Inner Responsibility for Outer Circumstances

67.

Celebrate Life

68.

Happiness as a Choice

69.

Freedom from Programmed Beliefs

70.

Give Yourself Credit

71.

Get in Touch with Your Heart

72.

Live Your Highest Truth

73.

Undaunted Perseverance

74.

Living with Reverence

75.

**Trusting in Benevolent
Outcomes**

76.

Divine Compassion

77.

**Balancing Proactive and
Receptive**

78.

Eliminating Prejudices

79.

Connecting with the Divine

80.

Neutral Response

81.

Allow Self-guidance

82.

Effortless Manifestation

83.

Focusing on Inner Peace

84.

Move Beyond Illusion

85.

Clarity of Thought

86.

Relaxed Awareness of Possibilities

87.

Choose the Quality of the Journey

88.

Accessing Subtle Information

89.

Enrichment through Diversity

90.

Supportive Environment

91.

Self-determined Well-being

92.

Fully Engaging

93.

**Changing Outcome through
Changed Attitudes**

94.

The Large Perspective

95.

Flourishing Gifts

96.

Being the Center of Influence

The Song of the 96 Tones Godhood

Song 6: The Song of Embracing the Paradox

1. Knowing the game of questions and answers to be a game we play in order to be self-directive in determining the course of the never-ending journey.

2. Equal appreciation for the valuable contribution of both opposite poles.

3. Boundless existence without the need for a reference point.

4. The release of the need for understanding by entering the paradox of indescribable existence.

5. Releasing the tension of linear time through releasing resistance to the unknowable.

6. Gaining comfort with the indescribable vastness of our being.

7. Fluid mastery of the ability to manifest the reality of choice through perspectives.

8. The removal of the judgments of opposites of mind, heart and spirit.

9. The overcoming of inertia by embracing oneness.

10. Dissolving the subatomic particles to dissolve the mirrors of existence.

11. Singing the seven tones of fertility through the honored expression of the feminine.

12. Approaching the mystery with reverent humility.

13. Becoming a participant in the perpetual alchemy of existence.

14. The release of the geometry of the tube torus by dissolving the matrix.

15. The metamorphoses of the ida and pingala through the integrated reunion of the feminine and masculine.

16. The freedom from the reliance on old energy sources through the first resurrection.

17. Individuation through unique perspective.

18. Becoming a cosmic energy source through the second resurrection.

19. Leveraged results through alchemy.

20. Embracing the contradiction.

21. Literacy in interpreting cosmic guidance.

22. The interdimensional tool of transcendence.

23. Allowing the contribution of diversity.

24. Governing your reality through self-government.

25. Purified emotions through increased perception.

26. The inspired life of full awareness.

27. Transcending opposition as a form of guidance.

28. Attracting possibilities through creating a space of unspecified hope.

29. Closing the gap between cause and effect by living in exponential time.

30. Becoming the source of inspiration through the influence of standing waveforms.

31. Compressing time through focusing on the details within the whole.

32. Clear membranes of the recapitulated life.

33. Self-sovereign supply of resources by the simultaneous expression of multi-perspectives.

34. Unique contribution through chosen perspectives.

35. The increase of resources through the interaction of fluid structure and disciplined flow.

36. Turning the unknowable into the known through vitality infused experiences.

37. Effortless knowing through humble acknowledgment of the unknowability of existence.

38. Uncompromising freedom from the beliefs of man.

39. Becoming the paradox by releasing value judgments.

40. Reserving resources through the genius of the silenced mind.

41. The timeless existence beyond the mirrors of life, death and ascension.

42. Releasing mediocrity by transcending past standards of excellence.

43. The unchallenged journey beyond the matrix through the negative resistance of transcendence.

44. Accessing the subtle currents of the inner senses.

45. Overcoming the addiction to the certitude of the known by releasing the need for a reference point.

46. Being at home in your vastness by knowing infinity to be in the details.

47. The full information exchange with the seven quantum fields of existence.

48. Potency through awareness of the interconnectedness of life.

49. The power source of inner growth stimulated by appreciative acceptance without.

50. Through fragility comes strength; through surrendered trust comes the power of the universe.

51. Only through living in the moment, do the secrets of the universe unfold.

52. Manifestation of immaculate timing through the regulating of the breath.

53. Inevitable creations through agendaless cooperation.

54. Coming home to the evolving core of humanness.

55. Restoring fluidity to the core of the DNA rose.

56. The activation of the third blood cell type, the black blood cells of the circulatory system.

57. The interpretation of interdimensional, subtle feelings through the black blood cells.

58. The living of the higher god archetypes to purify matrices and restore the pristine clarity of membranes.

59. Becoming a true elder of agelessness by living from multiple fields of perception at once.

60. Freedom from the control mechanisms that capture the minds of man through removing personal identities and beliefs.

61. Travelling the fluid journey of no beliefs.

62. The creation of a personal reality through opening a field of glad expectations.

63. The self-designed journey of grand adventure through aware discovery of the self in all.

64. Structured flow through integrating perception and emotion.

65. Being prepared for deep contentment and enjoyment of experiences.

66. Expecting immediate changes of grace in the environment by living your highest perception.

67. Turning ordinary moments into exceptional experiences.

68. Exemplifying the art of happiness.

69. Shedding personal matrices of conditioned behavior.

70. Basking in the nurturing glow of self-approval.

71. Living a spontaneous life of clear self-examination.

72. Courageous expression of your unique perspective.

73. Undaunted perseverance and optimism by recognizing the gifts of failure.

74. Honoring the sacred in all life.

75. Resting in the cradling arms of eternity.

76. Willingness to release prejudices through inclusive and compassionate understanding.

77. Becoming the active expression of the god and goddess archetypes.

78. Unified chakra field through releasing exclusivity and prejudices.

79. The holy alchemy of the cauldron of the heart.

80. Passive resistance through the imperviousness of the resonant fields.

81. The self-sovereignty of mastering tools of self-revelation.

82. Effortless manifestation through blending with Infinite Presence.

83. Becoming the embodiment of deep peace.

84. The purifying presence of the Haaraknit.

85. Perfect synchronicities of the immaculate mind.

86. Relaxing into infinite possibilities.

87. The freedom of choice of realities.

88. Mastering the fields of perception.

89. The alchemical blending of diverse ideologies.

90. The support system of fluid tribalism.

91. The moment of decision to choose happiness.

92. Multidimensional full presence in the moment.

93. Rewriting possibilities through a masterful act of magic.

94. The privilege of remembering the glory of the Source of Life.

95. The metamorphoses of the DNA into evolved capacities.

96. Undoing the tyranny of the assemblage point[10] through ascending the throne of self-determination.

---

[10] The assemblage point is a ball of light about the size of a fist, located an arm's length behind the heart and a little bit to the right. It determines our band of awareness, which reality we access. A slight movement of the assemblage point puts us in an altered state, such as meditation.

The Seven Steps of Mastery

Step 7

Mastering the Use and Practices of the Runes

Neither death, nor life, nor ascension can bind the one who remembers himself as a current in an eternal ocean.

~ Almine

The Field of Perception of the Unfolding Journey

The Wheel for the Runes of the Field of Perception of the Unfolding Journey

Keshet eresta misech uhasvi ska-urech nanat
Awaken and Integrate the Seven Fields of Perception

Fluid cooperation with the unfolding River of Life as guided by Infinite Intent is the hallmark of the Grand Master's perspective; the knowledge that truth is the ever new expression of life…

The Flow of the River of Intent

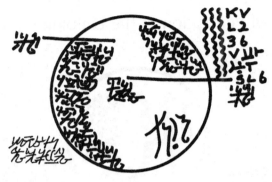

1.

Beyond the vale where flowers of separation grow
Beyond the valley where the River of Oneness flows
Lies the domain where no explanation goes
Where uncanvassed light eternally glows

2.

Time like tones, in swirls of color flows
Unbounded light flickers and glows
Shapes arise in fluid form
Like ocean waves from endlessness born

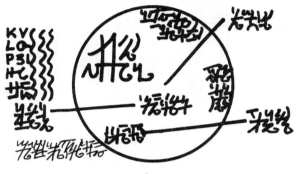

3.

No longer a puppet show controlled by lines
Free from bondage of space and time
Beyond the realms where opposites vie
Atomless matter unclustered lies

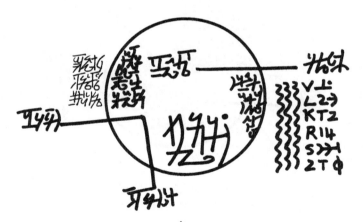

4.

Primordial matter, the realm of peace
The tension of form finally released
Fluid responses to Intent unheard
The Infinite's voice that as inspiration stirred

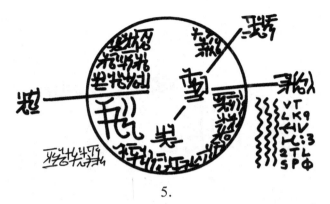

5.

What can you know of the journey that never ends
It cannot be known, but only be felt
Release self-reflection and the baggage of resistance
Become an aware explorer of existence

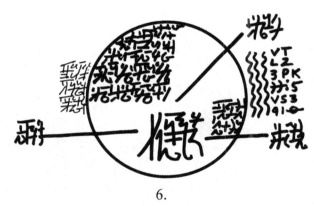

6.

Neither succumbing to oneness' allure
Or regarding the bliss as being more pure
Oneness and separation are opposites that have no place
When in holy communion, you touch the Infinite's face

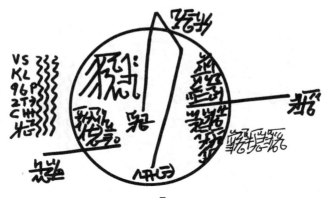

7.

A familiarity there is to the mirrors you have seen
A feeling of safety to go where you've been
Thus you surrender to a treadmill's pace
Where change takes place without any grace

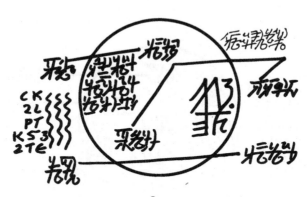

8.

No linear journey, are you eternally on
When within you, directions have merged as one
All that you can ever imagine to be
Already within and around you sleeps

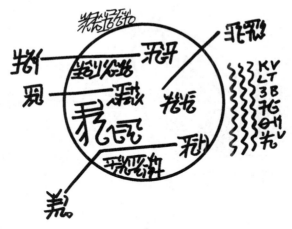

9.

With motionless motion, your awareness is spread
Not on a linear journey but standing waveforms instead
Whatever you choose is yours to take
Your journey through life is yours to make

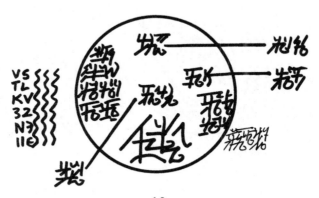

10.

Moonlight on water, sun on the lake
Poetry or dewdrops as the dawn breaks
It begins in the cells like a song not yet sung
Gently arriving, a new world has begun

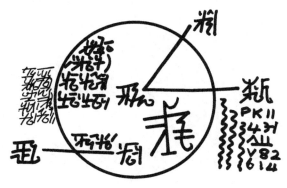

11.

First comes the dawning of light in the mind
Then a gilding compassion for all humankind
An irradiated countenance, too bright to see
A presence, a catalyst for all humanity

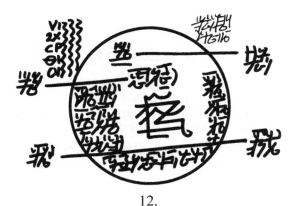

12.

Like a molecule of water that escapes into steam
First one, then the many, from matter break free
Returning to the original element before illusion reigned
The restoration of what once was, yet never the same

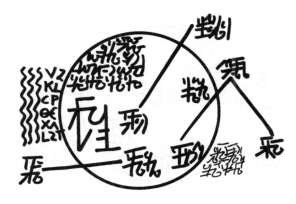

13.

Innocence lost, yet evolved expression gained
Refined appreciation of individuation's game
Sacred alchemy, a perpetual chain
Eternal resources the surrendered life can claim

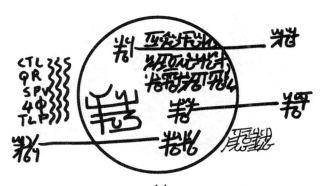

14.

Come follow the piper, the song of inspiration plays
How could we have known that inspiration and the
Infinite's voice is the same
Throw off the drama of the many, that attention claims
Or the seduction of the bliss and pristine existence remains

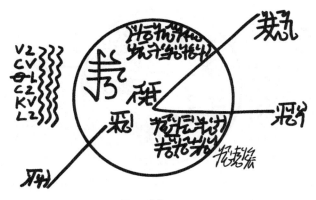

15.

Like the bud of a rose, protected and closed
The flowering of divinity hid where no one knows
Ignited by the voice of Divine, that through an open heart flows
Through graceful cooperation, our godhood unfolds

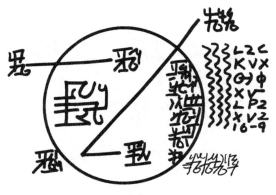

16.

With an inner light forms are aglow
Effortlessly, the inner senses know
A thunderous roar of liquid light
As newborn forms irradiate the night

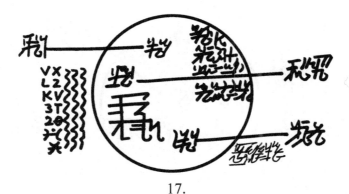

17.

An eternal romance unfolds like a rose
As cooperation with the Infinite grows
Silent guidance, a sensory response
Ripples within, materializes at once

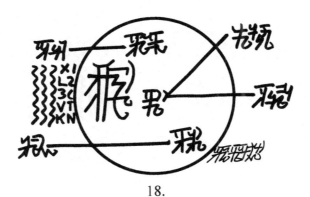

18.

A magical life, gladness of heart
In a mystical adventure, play your part
Upon the cosmic winds, seeds of delight
Spread their message as mind takes flight

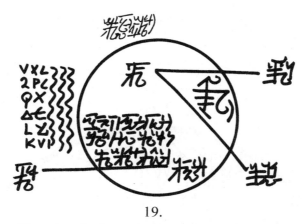

19.

Choose now the path that inspires your heart
Each an endless journey on a moving chart
Deep contentment, the need for outcome released
Disciplined boundlessness, continually increased

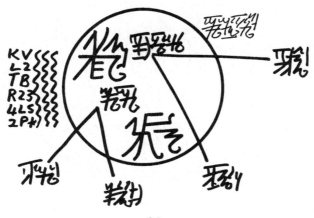

20.

A tribe of many no longer controls
As self-sovereign divinity eternally unfolds
Release the addiction to solid form
The never-ending journey's miracle is born

Manifested Life Map 1

The Map of Time for the Shamanic Perspective of the Known

Manifested Life Map 2

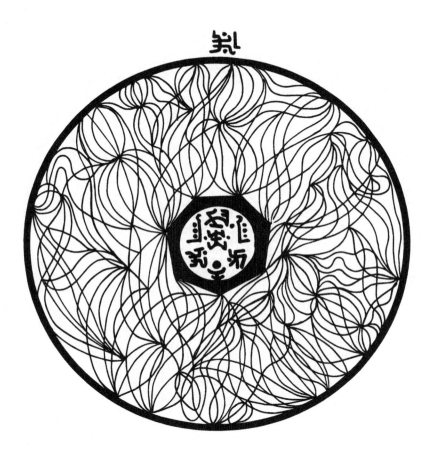

The Map of Time for the White Magic Perspective of the
Known

Manifested Life Map 3

The Map of Time for the Perspective of Healing of the Unknown

Manifested Life Map 4

The Map of Time for the Mystical Perspective of the Unknown

Preparing for Resurrection

1.
The 96 Tones of Confident Self-expression

The separation that exists between life, death, masculine and feminine realities is the result of 96 Tones of Confident Self-expression that are not being expressed. By restoring their expression, the division disappears and resurrection becomes possible. Resurrection is the goal of the Rune Master who bridges inner and outer space, death and life – by living both simultaneously. The incorporating of these 96 tones into our daily lives is essential for the Rune Master.

1. Knowing our capacities to be equal to the challenges.
2. Trusting the validity of our decisions.
3. Mastering self-doubt and fear by changing perspectives.
4. Confidence through automatic assisting of others.
5. Supporting our own dreams and desires.
6. Self-encouragement through giving ourselves credit for achievements.
7. Living prepared to be amazed at yourself.
8. Valuing our beingness as much as our doingness.
9. Unquestioning acceptance of inner knowing.
10. Releasing the need to be understood.
11. Knowing the purity and authenticity of our highest truth to benefit all life.
12. Confident trust in the value of our unique expression to the interconnectedness of life.
13. Trusting that we will effortlessly know what we need to do each moment.

14. Knowing the holiness of our being the expression of the One Life.

15. Confidence in our responses to inspiration.

16. Feeling secure with learning rather than knowing.

17. Confident acceptance of self-guidance through lack of clarity.

18. Moving confidently into the unknown beyond reason.

19. Automatic action through aligning with Infinite Intent.

20. Mature willingness to create the quality of the journey.

21. Embracing challenge as a doorway to a more evolved expression of our individuation.

22. Trusting the perfection of our choices.

23. Knowing the innocence of our existence.

24. Trusting that life responds to the power of our intent.

25. Finding our strength through our perceived weakness.

26. Confidently establishing the boundaries of our sacred personal space.

27. The confidence of living a higher reality amongst those of lesser consciousness.

28. Knowing my being to be my sustenance.

29. Confidently increasing personal resources through leaving one's comfort zone.

30. Trusting the flawlessness of my self-expression.

31. Confidently embracing the new experiences brought by change.

32. Trusting my ability to excel under pressure.

33. Self-appreciation of the miraculous beauty of my body.

34. Unselfconsciously excelling.

35. Welcoming the unpredictability of the adventure.

36. The wonderment of new discoveries through fluid and fresh perspectives.

37. The complete fulfillment of self-love.

38. Releasing fear of commitment through loving ourselves.

39. Embracing the exquisite lovability of my own being.

40. Trusting our ability to create with elegance from the potential of the moment.

41. Trusting our ability to manifest an abundant life.

42. Releasing agendas through self-sovereignty.

43. Trusting the guidance of that which inspires me.

44. Knowing yourself as the only being in your reality.

45. Knowing yourself as having the power to change your environment.

46. Living beyond the need for validation through self-validation.

47. Having the surrendered trust of an eternal perspective.

48. Living in reverent appreciation for life through self-appreciation.

49. Trusting my ability to find joy through authenticity.

50. Full awareness of the magic inherent in my being.

51. Being an intrepid and fearless explorer of the never-ending vastness of my being.

52. Trusting the benevolence and clarity of all aspects of my being.

53. Fully engaging the adventure of the unpredictable journey.

54. Stepping free from the false security of the prison bars of belief systems.

55. The complete willingness to leave the false security of the tribe.

56. The unbound freedom of releasing identities.

57. The courageous willingness to govern the world of your experience through self-government.

58. Releasing resistance through trust, to allow the fluid flow of Infinite Intent.

59. Cultivating emotional self-sovereignty through the full expression of the subpersonalities.

60. Releasing the bindings of need based interactions with others through living a self-fulfilled life.

61. Fluidly manifesting by releasing old belief systems.

62. Freedom of choice through living free of accommodating the expectations of others.

63. Fully trusting the subtle messages of inner senses.

64. Trust as a basis of making decisions, rather than fear.

65. Willingness to continually rebirth anew.

66. Willingness to express the magnificent fullness of our being without reservation.

67. Trusting our ability to speak freely without attachment to outcome.

68. Eliminating comparisons by eliminating self-reflection.

69. Allowing our greatness to shine by releasing the need for uniformity.

70. Feeling comfortable with living beyond the confines of the matrix.

71. Refusing to allow reason to second-guess intuitive knowing.

72. Having the strength to be vulnerable.

73. Living with the intimacy of an open heart.

74. Confidently presenting the fruits of our heartfelt labor.

75. Self-assuredly asking for whatever you want.

76. Fully accepting the unique standard of beauty of my body.

77. Facing obstacles with the confident knowing that they are gifts of perception.

78. Releasing the fear of getting lost in my own vastness.

79. Removing the illusion of risks by trusting our ability to create our own reality.

80. Feeling confident in our aloneness by being home for ourselves.

81. Feeling confident that whatever we release can be manifested again when needed.

82. Having the courage to live agelessly.

83. Removing fear of being overwhelmed by living in simplicity within complexity.

84. Confidently living in godhood.

85. Speaking from divine wisdom by removing the need to speak.

86. Living in the confident peace of being a tribe of one.

87. Confidently living in self-awareness while losing self-identity.

88. Feeling the self-generated safety of the self-sovereign life.

89. Confident knowing of the impeccable timing of the unfolding universe.

90. Confident, automatic and inevitable action through inner silence and surrendered trust.

91. Trusting the creativity of my inspired actions and creative solutions.

92. Respecting the holy resources of my being by refusing to let others drain it.

93. Confidence in my ability to live up to my vision and ideals.

94. Confidence in my ability to live beyond mortal boundaries.

95. Poise through self-mastery.

$$=$$

96. Steadfastly believing in that which I cannot prove, but know in my heart to be true.

The absolute confidence through the acceptance of the unseen perfection of life, that I can manifest heaven on Earth.

2.

Relocating the Life Force Center in the Heart

The highest evolutionary stage within separation consciousness is ascended mastery. The highest stage in resurrection is super godhood. During the second stage of oneness, the life force center moves from the navel to the heart in preparation for the super-god stage of resurrection.

The following exercise can be done at least twice a week for three months. Prepare for this by completing the activation of the God Merkaba.

Relocating the Life-force Center

Creating stacks

1. On the bottom of the stack place the **Sigil for the Life Force Center of the Navel**

2. On top of that place the **Sigil for the Relocation of the Life Center Center in the Heart**

3. On top of that place the **Sigil to Activate the Resurrection Acupuncture Point**

4. On top of the stack place the **Sigil for Opening the Navel Area and Purification of the Life Force Center**

5. **Hold a list of the Three Decisions in your hand as you lie on top of the stack.**

The Position of the Life Force Center in the God Kingdom and all Lower Stages of Evolution

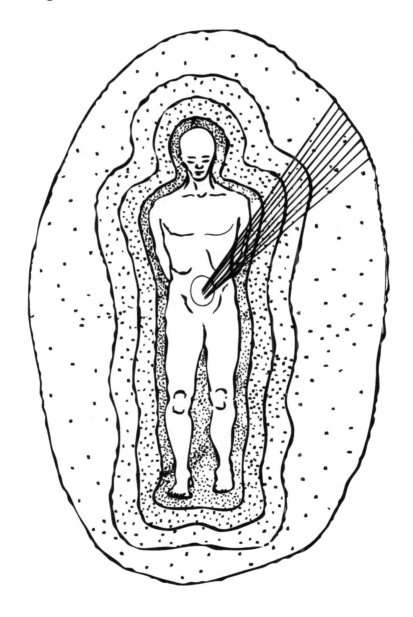

The Sigil to Activate the Resurrection Acupuncture Point

(Located approximately one inch above the navel)

The Sigil for the Life Force Center of the Navel

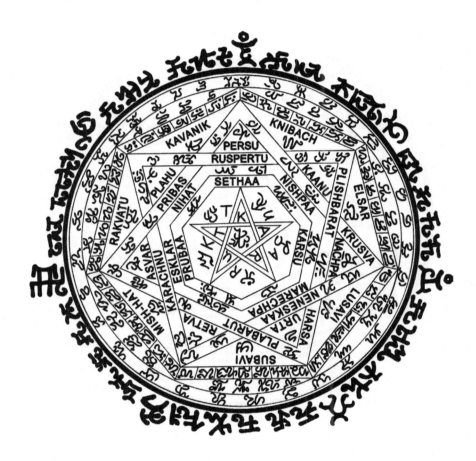

The Sigil for the Stable Relocation of the Life Force Center in the Heart

The Wheel for Opening the Navel Area and Purification of the Life Force Center

The Three Decisions

The commitments for a resurrected being

1. Can I leave the temptations of the world behind? The most common ones that bind us to the games of men are:
   - Greed
   - Lust
   - Jealousy
   - Duplicity/dishonesty
   - Gluttony
   - Slothfulness/laziness
   - Unkindness/lack of compassion
   - Looking for answers without/outside self

2. Can I dedicate my life to rising beyond mediocrity, to fly fearlessly like the eagle, leaving the flocks of birds behind? This question implies that we are willing to live without the tribe's approval and free from social conditioning.

3. Am I willing to take full responsibility for the quality of the journey and the conditions of my life, forsaking all self-pity and victimhood? Whatever is without is also within. Healing ourselves by changing attitudes, inner flawed perceptions and distorted emotions can heal the world.

Method

- Read the three decisions carefully while lying on the power wheels. Truly commit to them and envision how your life will change.
- When you are finished with integrating the 3 decisions, complete 3 deep breath cycles (inhale and exhale), while seeing the life force

center behind the navel center glowing brightly. (It is a bluish white ball of light about the size of a grapefruit.)
- On the fourth breath, cup both hands together under the life force center as through carrying it in your cupped hands.
- With the next long inbreath, raise it up from the navel to the heart and relax your hands. See it glow brightly in the middle of the heart center.

4. Activating Three Unused Areas of the Brain

The seemingly dormant areas of the brain: 1) Broca's area, 2) Wernicke's area and 3) the Planum Temporale deplete the pineal of its resources when dormant. The pineal is vital to the life of a resurrected being as it interprets much of the non-cognitive information received from our environment. When these three areas become active in an evolved being, they energize the pineal. Factors that affect their activation:
- The clearing of blockages from old programs in the eight extraordinary meridians is required. (See *Clearing of the 8 Extraordinary Meridians of the Body* set on http://fragrancealchemy.com)
- A commitment to the three decisions is required.
- The activation of the two resurrection acupressure points[11] is required: the one in the high heart and the one 1- inch above the navel. The high heart point in the center of the sternum is a trigger for the activation of the higher function of all 672 acupressure points – to convey information between inner and outer space.

---

[11] The alchemical oils for these points are available from Fragrance Alchemy htttp://fragrancealchemy.com. The navel point uses lotus oil and the high heart uses a Champaka blend.

5. Becoming Co-creators with Infinite Intent

The clearing and higher functioning of the eight meridians prepares us for forming without what inspires within. Boca's area, Wernicke's area and the Planum Temporale help us form inner spatial relationships for the external articulation of fluid form.

Four different layers of geometry form external shape: Projective geometry, Affine geometry, Metric geometry and Euclidian geometry. The four fields of geometry are related to the four points of the cross ratio. In every subsequent or higher layer of geometry, one point is moved to inner space – the mind or imagining of the observer. When we reach the fourth Euclidian layer, we have only one point remaining: the unity, the One.

The more the external is experienced as Oneness, the more complex the inner geometry becomes since the points have been moved to inner space. Images within inner space are experienced through the previously dormant three areas of the brain. Images within our mind are not the same as images within inner space. The latter are not seen with the mind's eye, but rather felt throughout the body. The forming of shape in inner space springs from Infinite stirrings of inspiration rather than remembered experiential associations. To know the unimagined magical worlds within is so begin to manifest it without.

The Sigil for the Activation of the Four Layers of Geometry of Inner Space

The Sigil for the Three-dimensional Gyroscope

Located at the bridge of the nose, it is an organ of discernment

Isabach

This evolving organ is the source of forming an up and a
down witihin the spacelessness of inner space.

The Sigil for the Activation of the Higher Functions of the Tongue to Relay the Heat Sensors of the Inner Senses

As interpreted by the last 15 Runes of Metaphysics (82-96)

The Sigil for the Activation of the Higher Function of the Nose to Relay Inner Senses of Smell.

As interpreted by the first 12 Runes of Godhood.

The activated inner smell can receive the higher pheromones that a god being emits.

Using the Seven Sets of Runes as a Method of Self-Guidance

What is the Source of Guidance

Within the rich inner infrastructure of man, a river of untapped potential awaits discovery. Like the Yin and the Yang, the inner and outer realities are opposites, divided by their inability to communicate in a mutually understandable way. This seemingly insurmountable language barrier can be overcome however, by developing a linguistic bridge that communicates between the inner and outer realities. Such a bridge is provided by the ancient traditions of the Runes.

The intent of someone seeking the wisdom of the cards creates a mutual agreement between their inner and outer realities that this is a system that will be the communication method of choice for the outer articulation of inner guidance. A rune representing a specific principle, desired by someone as an expression in his or her environment, can also send a reverse communication from their outer reality to the inner, eliciting support for its manifestation. Carrying a specific rune with us, reading its wisdom frequently and living its guiding principle, the inner potential of our being is alerted to its desirability so that it can aid in its manifestation.

How to Use the Runes for Guidance

Choosing a daily rune from any of the 7 sets of runes as a tool for guidance is helpful to provide an inspirational thought or to provide wisdom for a specific question that you have formed in your mind prior to choosing a rune from a container. You could use a different set for each day of the week. The rune you pick should be randomly drawn (you should not be able to see which rune you pick) and placed on the table facedown in front of you. Once you have placed it in position you may turn it over and look at it.

A spread of runes is utilized to provide clearer insights about obstacles to outcomes, as well as for learning what perception must be gained from a specific situation. To do this, the runes are mixed together (sets are always stored separately) and a certain number of them are drawn at random. The runes are then placed in a specific pattern. The order in which the rune is chosen from the container and placed facedown on the table (as indicated by the numerical order of the pattern or spread) is very important. This enables the accurate interpretation of the guidance.

Note: The directions are written for physical runes such as those painted on stones. These would be kept in a container that can be reached into. A simple alternative would be to print the runes of each set on cards that can be laminated and color-coded (follow the color scheme of the chakras with set one being red and set seven violet). If using cards, they should be shuffled and then spread facedown on a flat surface in order to draw one. The person asking for answers should always be the one to draw the rune card.

Why Spreads or Patterns are Necessary

The bridging language of inner and outer realities is symbolic. The rune itself is symbolic of forces at work in your life. So also is the spread that is used as a framework within which answers are received.

The inner information is fluid; an expression that the mind is unable to grasp. The spread's framework, and then the chosen runes as reference points, gives mind a starting point: an end to the golden thread that leads into the labyrinth. It must then unravel the mysteries of the messages of the runes by using reason and intuition.

In describing how to use patterns, or spreads of rune placement, for convenience the directions have been given for runes printed on cards. Please note that the reverse side of the rune sets cannot indicate whether the card drawn and placed is upside-down or not. An upside-down card is a valuable indicator of missing elements that will hinder the smooth unfoldment of events.

The Basic Spread uses only the first four sets of runes, drawing one rune from each. The Spread for gaining a Yes or No answer uses a rune card from each of the seven decks, as well as the card of the 96th rune of the 7th set of runes.

Working with the Spreads of Runes

1.
The Basic Spread

Envision the issue you desire clarity on within your mind.

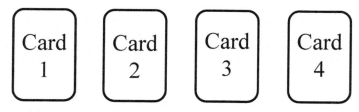

Place the 4 rune cards you have chosen one by one, face-up, in the order and position shown above.

Card 1: The Past
This card indicates what is leaving your life and how to adjust to the changes. The card of transformation.

Card 2: The Present
The challenge, or that which pertains to the question before you. The card of transmutation.

Card 3: The Future

The predicted outcome most likely to happen. The card of transfiguration.

Card 4: The Guidance

Clarity for how to proceed with your actions and responses. The card of transcendence.

2.

The Spread for Gaining a Yes or No Answer

Formulate a question that requires a specific yes or no answer within your mind.

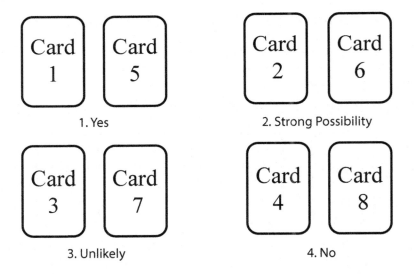

1. Yes   2. Strong Possibility

3. Unlikely   4. No

Directions
- Remove card number 96 of the 7ᵗʰ set of runes from the deck and set it aside facedown. Shuffle each of the decks of cards separately and lay them facedown on the table.
- Select 7 cards, one card from each set of runes.
- Shuffle card number 96 and the 7 cards together, until you no longer know which card is number 96.

- Drawing one card at a time, place it in the order as illustrated.
- The outcome will be indicated by whichever grouping of cards includes number 96. For instance, when card number 96 shows up in the third group of cards, the outcome you desire is unlikely to happen.

Can the Outcome be Changed

In the spread for gaining a yes or no answer, the chosen card that ends up positioned next to card number 96 indicates what insight is needed to change the outcome to a beneficial one. It must also be remembered that living the moment well, very directly impacts your future and the cards are representing that which is required to do so.

The cards in the Basic Spread offer insights that affect:

1. What needs to be released – the Past
2. What is needed to meet the challenge – the Present
3. What is needed for the self-determined manifestation of graceful outcomes – the Future
4. What responses are needed to take the correct steps upon the journey of unfoldment – the Guidance

No future outcome is unchangeable in the way that it has to unfold. Our life's journey can be one of grace or one of opposition. There are many choices along the broad highways of the Infinite and within the grand design of life. The self-guidance facilitated by the sacred tool of the Runes is a valuable tool to help us choose wisely.

Manifesting Beneficial Outcomes
in Harmony with Infinite Intent

The Invitation to the Alchemist
Plus
Answers to Guide the Journey
through Ceremonial Spreads

Introduction

The Runes are not only a tool of guidance but also a manifestation device. The ceremony for **Manifesting Beneficial Outcomes in Harmony with Infinite Intent** is done to clear the field of intent of any obstructive thought forms. The ceremony uses a form of high alchemy in which the practitioner is part of the equation. It provides a 'blank canvas' for manifestation. Leave the stack of wheels you have used for this ceremony undisturbed.

The next step is to form intent as to what it is you wish to manifest. To envision it, see it taking place on the screen of your mind, inside your forehead. Feel it with gratitude as if it is already there. Then silently formulate the question: What is needed to manifest this outcome?

The third step is to choose a rune card from each of the following sets of runes in the following order:

1. Set 1
2. Set 2
3. Set 5
4. Set 6
5. Set 7

Place them on the corresponding numbers around the outside of the **Wheel to Strengthen the Outcome** on top of the stack you used in the ceremony.

Examine the cards that have been drawn. Their specific relevance in manifestation is indicated by the position on the wheel – for instance, card 1 addresses relationships involved in the question. The presence of upside-down cards when using runes for manifestation purposes must be immediately addressed.

Upside-down Cards

Find where the principal of the upside-down card is missing or distorted within you. Do the introspective self-work to change it by changing your perspective. When you feel that this has been successfully done, turn the card right-side up.

Go through the cards one by one, and feel each of the principles within you radiating out into your environment. Envisions it affecting the manifestation of your intent beneficially.

Close with the words:

I contribute my unique perspective to the Infinite's Intent. May the pure desires of my heart thrive through perpetual alchemy.

The Wheel of Magic of the God Kingdom

Provides Guidance on Potentialities

Charavech Hikva Menenuch Sevatu

Open the Gates of Impeccable Magic

Revealing the Potential of the Main Aspects of a Situation

The Sigil of the Real High Heart

Provides Guidance for your Response to the Situation for Highest Outcome

The Wheel to Strengthen the Outcome

The high alchemy is a centrifugal standing waveform, inspired by the motionless motion of the Infinite.

Answers to Guide the Journey

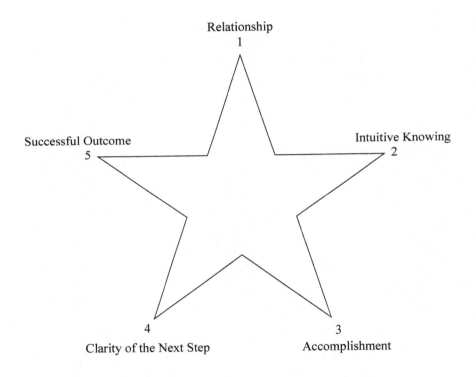

This overlay applies to wheels

Small Wheel 1

Wheel of Magic of the God
Kingdom

Small Wheel 2

Wheel of Magic of the God
Kingdom

Small Wheel 3

Wheel of Magic of the God
Kingdom

Small Wheel 4

Wheel of Magic of the God
Kingdom

Small Wheel 5

Wheel of Magic of the God
Kingdom

Note: The wheels are placed on the corresponding numbers around the Wheel of Magic of the God Kingdom.

Small Wheel 1
Sigil of the Real High Heart

Small Wheel 2
Sigil of the Real High Heart

Small Wheel 3
Sigil of the Real High Heart

Small Wheel 4
Sigil of the Real High Heart

Small Wheel 5
Sigil of the Real High Heart

Note: The wheels are placed around the outside of the Sigil of the Real High Heart, on the corresponding numbers.

The Five Core Principles of Pristine Man

1. Loving unconditionally without pain
2. Effortless knowingness respected
3. The awakening of unarticulated qualities within the self through the aware appreciation of other's enlightened qualities
4. Courageously choosing what inspires
5. Self-sovereign commitment to excellence

Prayer for Using the Sigil of the High Heart

May my body and the greater body of my environment, become the receiving cauldron for the sacred alchemy of Infinite Intent and the resonant response it evokes within me.

Savech sesabi uret viblachvi harunes

May excellence flourish through cooperative oneness

Note: A cauldron is the alchemist's term for the area in which the alchemy takes place.

Protocol for the Manifesting of Beneficial Outcomes in Harmony with Infinite Intent

Tools:

1. Wheel of Magic of the God Kingdom plus the 5 small wheels that accompany it.

2. The Sigil of the Real High Heart plus the 5 small wheels that accompany it.

3. The Wheel to Strengthen the Outcome

4. The 5 Core Principles of Pristine Man

5. The Prayer for Using the Sigil of the Real High Heart

Method:

Create a center stack upon which you will lie. This stack is placed behind the navel as you lie down. You may laminate the wheels to protect them for repeated use.

- On the bottom place the *Wheel of Magic of the God Kingdom*. Around it, place the *5 small wheels for the Wheel of Magic* at the relevant positions.

- Next place the *Sigil of the Real High Heart* with the *5 small wheels for the Sigil of the Real High Heart* in the appropriate positions

- On top of the Sigil for the Real High Heart, place the *Wheel to Strengthen the Outcome*.

- As you start the ceremony, have the *5 Core Principles of Pristine Man* and the *Prayer for the Sigil of the Real High Heart*.

Prior to doing the ceremony, the Principles should be contemplated and meditated upon so that you become very familiar with them.

During the ceremony consider each principle one at a time. Feel the intent of the principle rippling out from you as a centrifugal standing waveform throughout the cosmos. As it ripples throughout the cosmos, feel the feeling move through you and your environment as well.

When you have completed all 5 Principles, close the ceremony with the Prayer for the Real High Heart. This is your response upon being inspired by Infinite Intent.

You are asking the Infinite's Intent to be strongly coming through the ceremony, through you, through your environment, and you are responding to it in harmony. You have become the place where alchemy takes place between the Great Alchemist, which is the Infinite Being, and yourself, creating a new form of expression.

When you have completed the ceremony, with gratitude and respect, you are ready to work with the Rune's Ceremonial Spreads.

The Five Core Principles

The Five Core Principles represent the 585 Principles of Pristine Humanity that are like the pillars of the temple of pristine man's reality – a reality so much higher than what it has become, beyond our imagination.

1) Loving Unconditionally without Pain

    The first principle is Loving Unconditionally without Pain. If you have looked previously, for example, what it is that would make you truly see that, you might come to the conclusion that it is the realization that our journey is eternal. Some come, some go, but over the span of thousands and hundreds of thousands and beyond years of immortal life, you hold on lightly – you love impersonally, and you emphasize within the impersonal love the uniqueness of specific relationships. You are filled, you are full, you are all things that are within Infinite Life in microcosmic form. Love, then, has no agenda.

    Understand these things before you lie down. Once you can feel that feeling of being in such a state of godhood that all things are loved by you, feel this rippling out through you in a centrifugal standing wave – in other words, you are the center point, you are that pebble that falls in the pond, and it ripples out from you in rings going throughout the entire cosmos. Although, at this point, you have let go of the image of the situation that you are specifically involved in, you know that whatever the situation may be, you are doing far more than just giving the situation these rings of influence. It is for all individuated life.

2) Effortless Knowing Respected

    The world believes that you need a college degree, 'or a this, or a that', in order for them to take one seriously. So, Effortless

Knowingness might seem inevitably present for you, but others demand that you explain it. Do not allow the cynics of the world to pull you out of believing your Effortless Knowingness and respecting the inevitable clarity of your next step, a place where mind cannot go, and intelligence cannot justify. Once you feel this, allow those ripples to go forth from you throughout all individuated life, where you are truly a being as vast as the cosmos, and this is but the central point of setting the motionless motion of a standing waveform into action. You are the harp that the Infinite is playing, but your music that you make with this – your action that you take to emit this pure frequency and light of these Five Core Principles – is the harpist that plays the harp strings of your environment, just the way you are played into music by the master harpist.

3) The awakening of unarticulated qualities within the self through the aware appreciation of other's enlightened qualities

4) Courageously choosing what inspires

   Much is expected from us, much is demanded from us. Choose what inspires you. If you are earning a living in your job and it does not inspire you, allow yourself immediately to start looking for another. But until that other inspiring job is achieved, allow yourself to find inspiration where you are. Bloom where you are planted. Be inspired where you are, and search for what inspires you.

5) Self-sovereign commitment to excellence

   It doesn't matter if there are others around to see you: The flower that blooms high up in a cave such as the Edelweiss in the mountains of Switzerland. Does it ask whether anyone can be that high up in the snow and ice to see it blossom? Wherever you are, let your actions be ones of devotion to life, and a celebration of the divinity of yourself. Self-sovereign, you will shine, whether others can see your light or not, for you are committed to being all that you can be.

Answers to Guide the Journey through Ceremonial Spreads

The following spreads are created by setting up the same stack of wheels as used in the manifestation ceremony. The spread is then created as instructed and placed on top of the stack. The empowering influence of the power wheels beneath the spread greatly enhances the clarity of purpose for which the spread was created. This can be used for all other more complex spreads.

Optional: To further enhance clarity for guidance for your next steps, the 144 names of the Angels of Clarity can be called out, briefly glancing at the sigil of each as you do so. Request their assistance with establishing clarity in your journey.

The Ceremonial Spreads of the Runes

1.

The Communication Spread

This spread is used for negotiations, arbitrations and communications. Instructions are given as though the runes are printed onto cards: Place 8 cards on the table as shown below, number 1-7 are drawn from rune sets 1-7. The 8th card is also drawn from the 7th set of runes.

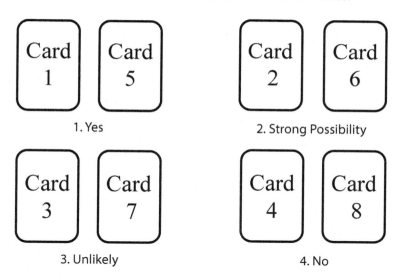

1. Yes   2. Strong Possibility

3. Unlikely   4. No

In communication, we are dealing with each other's subpersonalities. Communications often break down because we try to only communicate adult to adult. The child requires fun, spontaneity and enthusiasm. The nurturer requires a pleasant quality to the journey and a feeling of support. The sage or elder wants to know that there is a result of significance that will change lives for the better, and that there is fairness. The warrior demands self-respect and acknowledgment of his strong suits and that sacrifices will work for the good of all.

Taking the requirements of the subpersonalities into consideration, consider how the cards you have drawn are guiding you to interact with one another. Upside-down cards require work on your own subpersonality for success to occur. Be aware that in groups that have been together for a time (several months at least), individuals within the group will often play the role of these subpersonalities. The cards will also help with this situation.

2.
The Weekly Prediction Spread

The trend of a week can be predicted by this 7 card spread. The runes will indicate which attitudes need to be cultivated; which perceptions need to be required for a graceful journey through the week.

Upside-down cards will indicate where self-work is needed to beneficially affect your environment. One card for each day is chosen from each of the 7 sets of runes. When an upside-down card is drawn in this particular spread, the quality of the card preceding it should also be reassessed. Then work on the aspect within that the upside-down card represents. The reason this is done is that the spread represents a flow from one quality into another. The days affect one another.

Insert images of cards in clockwise order, starting at 12 noon with card 1, card 6 to the left of card 1, and card 7 in the center of all the cards. *Circular spreads are always drawn and laid out in a clockwise manner.*

Tones and Angels of Clarity

1. Tone of Clarity: Action integrated with highest knowing

    Angel: *Sihu-achvastret*

2. Tone of Clarity: Compassionate acceptance

    Angel: *Mestu-hurnahet*

3. Tone of Clarity: The fluid acceptance of the unknown

    Angel: *Vister-usutvi*

4. Tone of Clarity: Changing the past by changing the future

    Angel: *Herestat-narnuve*

5. Tone of Clarity: The comfortable mastery of grief

    Angel: *Kiher-astravu*

6. Tone of Clarity: Embracing the adventure of unforeseen outcomes

    Angel: *Viresat-manechve*

7. Tone of Clarity: Knowing the innocence of all experience

    Angel: *Suvilestret-arsta*

8. Tone of Clarity: Participation in the fluidly unfolding journey

    Angel: *Manurik-satve*

9. Tone of Clarity: Fully accepting all parts of ourselves as valid

   Angel: *Kisarutret*

10. Tone of Clarity: The acknowledged bounty of the moment

    Angel: *Velesh-manuvech*

11. Tone of Clarity: Complete transparency through knowing the flawlessness of existence

    Angel: *Sersanenuvet*

12. Tone of Clarity: Immediate forgiveness through and eternal perspective

    Angel: *Siharasat-erchbi*

13. Tone of Clarity: The deep peace of acknowledged self-sovereignty

    Angel: *Neskluset-vabrich*

14. Tone of Clarity: Full presence in the fulfillment of the present

    Angel: *Kahurnava-suhit*

15. Tone of Clarity: Honoring the validity of all experience

    Angel: *Plestrat-plavir*

16. Tone of Clarity: The foundation of eternal presence

    Angel: *Eresunavet*

17. Tone of Clarity: The appreciation of receptive states of being

    Angel: *Kihur-sarsanet*

18. Tone of Clarity: Trusting effortless answers of inevitability

    Angel: *Pesterut-mestu*

19. Tone of Clarity: Living beyond the sub-created reality of comparisons

    Angel: *Asbach-helsetvi*

20. Tone of Clarity: The expressed majesty of our infinite self through finite experiences

    Angel: *Nenusatra-ubich*

21. Tone of Clarity: Changing our environment by changing ourselves

    Angel: *Katru-arasvi*

22. Tone of Clarity: Uncompromising self-presence and support

    Angel: *Mesenek-plavi*

23. Tone of Clarity: The integrated contribution of our sub-personalities

    Angel: *Ertu-sarsanat*

24. Tone of Clarity: Acknowledged hopes and desires of the self

    Angel: *Kuhistra-babaru*

25. Tone of Clarity: Consciousness through conserving resources

    Angel: *Nenesilaver-aruta*

26. Tone of Clarity: Releasing expectations of timing through acknowledged timelessness

    Angel: *Kuhubit-aranus*

27. Tone of Clarity: Effective activity through the guidance of the silent mind

    Angel: *Keveter-rusavi*

28. Tone of Clarity: Grateful acknowledgment of present blessings

    Angel: *Bilestrahit-ursta*

29. Tone of Clarity: Embracing all things as an extension of ourselves

    Angel: *Mekparut-michter*

30. Tone of Clarity: Knowing the harmlessness of life

    Angel: *Huvares-elstaru*

31. Tone of Clarity: Mobilizing cosmic support through clear intent

    Angel: *Pekparus-skeleva*

32. Tone of Clarity: Non-attached enjoyment of the journey

    Angel: *Rutvarek-piresta*

33. Tone of Clarity: Passionate participation in creating the quality of experience

Angel: *Nensubaret-echta*

34. Tone of Clarity: Know the past as a fluidly changing reflection of the present

Angel: *Akverastu-mesenek*

35. Tone of Clarity: The timeless knowingness of our being as the source of our actions

Angel: *Para-erestavit*

36. Tone of Clarity: Changing disempowerment to mastery by altering perspective

Angel: *Kelsta-bibarech*

37. Tone of Clarity: Relinquishing external need fulfillment through chosen self-sovereignty

Angel: *Nensaru-kavavit*

38. Tone of Clarity: Committed appreciative perspectives

Angel: *Ukparesvi-meseklut*

39. Tone of Clarity: Acknowledged inspiration through increased awareness

Angel: *Kahurespahur-avesta*

40. Tone of Clarity: Grateful recognition of life beyond mortal boundaries

Angel: *Nansahur-trechvar*

41. Tone of Clarity: Trusting the resilient recovery beyond the experience of negative emotions

    Angel: *Suvahit-erstuvar*

42. Tone of Clarity: Knowing the benign nature of existence

    Angel: *Neneparus-stavir*

43. Tone of Clarity: Releasing the golden chains of good deeds done with the intent to save

    Angel: *Kusanar-stechvi*

44. Tone of Clarity: The courageous acknowledgment of buried emotions through the eternal perspective

    Angel: *Sirsanet-plustavar*

45. Tone of Clarity: The acknowledged power of being the center of your reality

    Angel: *Averekvi-manusta*

46. Tone of Clarity: Changing stagnation through embracing the new

    Angel: *Ekparu-selsaruvi*

47. Tone of Clarity: Humble mastery through acknowledging the unknowable nature of existence

    Angel: *Kiharesta-master*

48. Tone of Clarity: Eliminating overwhelm by focusing on the clarity of the next step

    Angel: *Aruselsavi-akvar*

49. Tone of Clarity: Knowing there is no point of arrival in an eternal existence

    Angel: *Menehik-parastu*

50. Tone of Clarity: The openness of a silent mind and unattached heart

    Angel: *Siheresat-kavenu*

51. Tone of Clarity: Embracing the flow of a non-egoic life

    Angel: *Trubilestar-parsetu*

52. Tone of Clarity: Know the bad in life as experiences in which the perfection is only partially seen

    Angel: *Vires-arabachvi*

53. Tone of Clarity: Moving beyond programs of punishment

    Angel: *Nesta-bilestur*

54. Tone of Clarity: The eternal adventurous quest of self-knowledge

    Angel: *Salsarut-mestahit*

55. Tone of Clarity: Knowing the unalienable right to be part of nature

    Angel: *Skrabaratur-mistel*

56. Tone of Clarity: Awakening the instinctual knowledge of the boundlessness of self

    Angel: *Pelshtrek-vatur*

57. Tone of Clarity: Evolving relationship as integrated oneness

    Angel: *Erasturabit-skravatur*

58. Tone of Clarity: Knowing the self's eternal being to be our sustenance

    Angel: *Usbar-menesuchvi*

59. Tone of Clarity: Faith in the infallibility of our choices

    Angel: *Ekspelenur-seresat*

60. Tone of Clarity: Knowing all beings to be incomprehensible expressions of eternity

    Angel: *Rutpelenor-verasvi*

61. Tone of Clarity: Dissipating anger through gaining inspiration

    Angel: *Neska-klesbasur*

62. Tone of Clarity: Dissipating pain through finding the poetry

    Angel: *Nuhuru-eresutva*

63. Tone of Clarity: Dissipating fear through an eternal perspective

    Angel: *Prisbelenus-savir*

64. Tone of Clarity: Dissipating guilt through seeing the eternal adventure

    Angel: *Aruk-spahurasa*

65. Tone of Clarity: Living free from nostalgic value judgments

    Angel: *Visterenut-ubechvi*

66. Tone of Clarity: Releasing the need for a point of arrival on an eternal journey

    Angel: *Eseklut-petrehir*

67. Tone of Clarity: Knowing all discovery to be self-discovery

    Angel: *Nanarus-usabi*

68. Tone of Clarity: Releasing the quest for uniformity by living beyond the tribe

    Angel: *Kavarut-plisatur*

69. Tone of Clarity: Dissolving intolerance by appreciating diversity

    Angel: *Sahit-elesubiva*

70. Tone of Clarity: Knowing that reduced ability in one area must be compensated for by increased ability elsewhere

    Angel: *Nachbar-ararut*

71. Tone of Clarity: Self-encouragement through acknowledging accomplishment

    Angel: *Sarut-aresutravar*

72. Tone of Clarity: Humility as the beginning of new discovery

    Angel: *Maraklut-miresvi*

73. Tone of Clarity: Unquestionable optimism for living through appreciative perspectives

    Angel: *Urastar-hechvaru*

74. Tone of Clarity: Virility through self-exploration with ruthless honesty

    Angel: *Minuher-maspahit*

75. Tone of Clarity: Inspired creativity through silence of the mind

    Angel: *Skavarut-elsachvi*

76. Tone of Clarity: Effortless knowing as the source of genius

    Angel: *Nistar-pelsavar*

77. Tone of Clarity: Vanquishing illusion by changing perspective

    Angel: *Hurutvi-skrihater*

78. Tone of Clarity: The bold courage of leaving the tribe behind

    Angel: *Velespahur-skelavit*

79. Tone of Clarity: Recognizing the enjoyment of masterfully wielding the tools of life

    Angel: *Runahit-mechtu*

80. Tone of Clarity: The dance of life guided by inspiration rather than pressure

    Angel: *Akvar-rutvrebi*

81. Tone of Clarity: Uncompromising self-value by knowing innate sacredness

    Angel: *Minavich-selsetu*

82. Tone of Clarity: The sacred journey of life through reverential awe

    Angel: *Estruhit-perenach*

83. Tone of Clarity: Disacknowledging the tyrannies of bodily systems

    Angel: *Ruvahit-paratu*

84. Tone of Clarity: Disacknowledging the unfounded certainty of others that they can know you

    Angel: *Sitrevis-barachvi*

85. Tone of Clarity: The purification of the sub-conscious mind through renewed perspective

    Angel: *Kuvitar-kelenis*

86. Tone of Clarity: Knowing perception to be the fullest use of compassionate understanding

    Angel: *Trabis-arunasvi*

87. Tone of Clarity: The involvement of the heart in the interpretation of experience

    Angel: *Seksaranit-havatur*

88. Tone of Clarity: Dissipating ghosts and impressions from the past by being fully present in the moment

    Angel: *Nansurak-plihestar*

89. Tone of Clarity: Knowing the boundlessness of the moment as timelessness

    Angel: *Kusbaru-nensurek*

90. Tone of Clarity: The release of identities associated with emotions, deeds, capacities or beliefs

    Angel: *Karanech-sitruher*

91. Tone of Clarity: Mastering the ability to regenerate our reality

    Angel: *Arekbar-setranut*

92. Tone of Clarity: The deep contentment of recognized infallibility

    Angel: *Kiruter-salsavi*

93. Tone of Clarity: Enjoying the effortless manifestation of creative solutions

    Angel: *Naspahur-sarasach*

94. Tone of Clarity: Releasing expectations and judgments through connecting essence to essence

    Angel: *Uruta-sereksu*

95. Tone of Clarity: Delightful interaction within undifferentiated love

    Angel: *Nansurata-bliser*

96. Tone of Clarity: Uncompromising emphasis of higher life

    Angel: *Rusata-mesetrut*

97. Tone of Clarity: Inevitable actions from non-cognitive knowing of the larger perspective

    Angel: *Kavech-nusbara*

98. Tone of Clarity: Clarity through releasing value judgments

    Angel: *Rutvelestra-parut*

99. Tone of Clarity: Living the qualities of godhood

    Angel: *Kevech-parus*

100. Tone of Clarity: Replacing the entanglements of man by being true to the self

    Angel: *Bilshpereta-manus*

101. Tone of Clarity: Allowing the opening of higher interpretive functions through releasing expectations

    Angel: *Kevech-sihustrar*

102. Tone of Clarity: Expecting joyful metamorphosis

    Angel: *Kelpahur-mirusat*

103. Tone of Clarity: Freedom from the perspective of being the victim of circumstances

    Angel: *Skrahuvit-arestu*

104. Tone of Clarity: Creative freedom of choice to respond to the currents of life

    Angel: *Melseranut-skruvi*

105. Tone of Clarity: Creating a joyous journey through inner emphasis

Angel: *Briharana-selsatu*

106. Tone of Clarity: Glorious allies of external support for inner emphasis

Angel: *Uvabich-miseretu*

107. Tone of Clarity: Restoring the magic of godhood by reclaiming the Earth's higher reality

Angel: *Keresutravit-skelerus*

108. Tone of Clarity: High perspective of praise and trust

Angel: *Arek-pelesar*

109. Tone of Clarity: Vision coupled with confident knowledge of self-empowerment

Angel: *Mitra-velestur*

110. Tone of Clarity: Ascending the throne of being the center of your reality

Angel: *Mensech-uhururarat*

111. Tone of Clarity: The unclouded vision of trusting peace

Angel: *Sihar-ublechsvi*

112. Tone of Clarity: The majestic alliance with Infinite Intent

Angel: *Nensurat-arabi*

113. Tone of Clarity: The activation of full DNA capacity

Angel: *Mestur-kestrachvi*

114. Tone of Clarity: The expectation of life's magic revealing itself

Angel: *Sekrenut-alestar*

115. Tone of Clarity: Seeing with the wonderment of a child

Angel: *Hechvaravi-menes*

116. Tone of Clarity: The unbiased feeling of a self-fulfilled life

Angel: *Karastar-seravi*

117. Tone of Clarity: The uncompromising reverence for the self as everything

Angel: *Viravelesvi-karas*

118. Tone of Clarity: The restoration of perception's song

Angel: *Merenech-suvi*

119. Tone of Clarity: The gentle guidance of the song of the self

Angel: *Klisaver-aravi*

120. Tone of Clarity: Replacing the two-dimensional reality of man with the virtual reality of godhood

Angel: *Vruhes-arasta*

121. Tone of Clarity:
Re-acquaintance with the
innocence of pristine existence

Angel: *Neserech-pluhaster*

122. Tone of Clarity: Appreciation
as a filter for empathy

Angel: *Kavanas-parahur*

123. Tone of Clarity: The
unshakable knowing of the
perfection of the totality of
experience

Angel: *Narastu-viprahat*

124. Tone of Clarity: The pristine
emotions of high vision

Angel: *Kerus-abechspi*

125. Tone of Clarity: The deep
contentment of endlessness

Angel: *Sutri-eretarava*

126. Tone of Clarity: The
rediscovery of the self through
perpetual revelations

Angel: *Kunes-siharavat*

127. Tone of Clarity: Marveling at
the miracle of boundless living

Angel: *Ustar-eksuravi*

128. Tone of Clarity: Self-confident
exploration of the eternal
adventure

Angel: *Meleruk-haraspi*

129. Tone of Clarity: Unclouded discernment of the direction of the dance

Angel: *Mitrutet-asaranat*

130. Tone of Clarity: Uncovering the ecstatic artistry of existence

Angel: *Kenesur-blivarus*

131. Tone of Clarity: The self-fulfilled life of tonal luminosity

Angel: *Vesetre-kubavis*

132. Tone of Clarity: Enthusiastic participation in the endless surprises of life

Angel: *Urukpater-misuret*

133. Tone of Clarity: Perpetual self-regeneration through the release of memories

Angel: *Elstavi-vriberestu*

134. Tone of Clarity: The release of potential through exponential time

Angel: *Kuprahit-aksterenu*

135. Tone of Clarity: Becoming the contradiction of knowing the unknowable

Angel: *Uplarut-meskuravet*

136. Tone of Clarity: Endless alchemical love affair

Angel: *Akvraster-hurubar*

137. Tone of Clarity: Exhilaration through refined awareness

Angel: *Husatar-mirabes*

138. Tone of Clarity: Assuaging the longing for home through the indivisible element

Angel: *Urchklater-sibahus*

139. Tone of Clarity: The deep peace of the self-directed journey

Angel: *Esebet-praspata*

140. Tone of Clarity: Emphasis through deliberately directed questions

Angel: *Rutsklaher-suvesvi*

141. Tone of Clarity: The purification of life through appreciative perspectives

Angel: *Nureruk-sitretva*

142. Tone of Clarity: Replacing work and duty with passionate self-expression

Angel: *Etrebit-plisatut*

143. Tone of Clarity: The unselfconscious ascension beyond the matrix of the masses

Angel: *Neserut-plabit*

144. Tone of Clarity: Powerful existence through the integration of inner and outer space

Angel: *Eksaver-skrivanach*

The Runes of the Unfolding Journey

The Runes of the Field of Perception of the Unfolding Journey

The Runes of The Living Library

For ages seers have spoken of life as being a dream, experienced in the tube torus as the in- and out- breath of the Infinite. This rotating tube torus has served as an incubation chamber for individuations, a womb in which the embryo slumbers and dreams.

This book, and particularly the revelation of the seventh set of runes, heralds a time when the birth of life outside the womb, the awakening, is at hand. The principles represented by the runes are the deeply profound keys to the awakening beyond the dream. Their levels of mystery should not be underestimated, nor should they be taken at face value. They hold within them the secrets of the fluid construction of a reality of empowered self-determination for the awakened individual.

The 96 Runes of the Living Library

1.

Effortless Progress

2.

A Larger Perspective

3.

Exceeding Expectations

4.

Accept What Mind Cannot Control

5.

Knowing the Origins of Your Actions

6.

Following Inspiration

7.

Full Commitment

8.

A Window of Opportunity

9.

Conscious Choices

10.

Effortless Solutions

11.

Releasing Past Expectations

12.

Seizing Possible Opportunities

13.

Dramatic Change

14.

Beneficial Partnerships

15.

Honesty with Yourself

16.

The Artistic Expression

17.

Power Source

18.

**Release Attempts to Control
Results**

19.

A Pivotal Moment

20.

Divine Inspiration

21.

Creativity

22.

Artful Expressions

23.

Empowerment

24.

Inner Knowingness

25.

Leveraged Results

26.

Vitality

27.

Clear Perception

28.

Cooperative Communication

29.

Fluid Compassion

30.

Contributions of Partnership

31.

Following Your Heart

32.

Evolving to the Next Stage

33.

Choosing Self-sovereignty

34.

Taking Responsibility

35.

Work Together

36.

Seeing Beyond the Distortion

37.

Non-conformity

38.

Self-expression

39.

Releasing Old Belief Systems

40.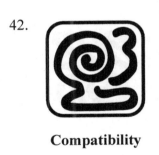

Increased Capacity

41.

Graceful Change

42.

Compatibility

43.

Authentic Expression

44.

Self-empowered Contribution

45.

Full Acceptance

46.

Rising Above Mediocrity

47.

Read the Signs of the Environment

48.

Flexibility

49.

Supportive Assistance

50.

New Potential

51.

Maintaining Hope

52.

Surpassed Expectations

53.

Discovering Wisdom

54.

Self-confident Knowing

55.

Open Receptivity

56.

Interpreting Subtle Information

57.

Receiving Blessings

58.

Expecting Miracles

59.

Transience

60.

Enjoy the Journey

61.

Focus on the Details

62.

Embracing Change

63.

Guidance from the Dreamtime

64.

Freedom from Belief Systems

65.

Discerning Choices

66.

Surprising Unfoldments

67.

Reaping Rewards

68.

Guiltless Journey

69.

A Love Affair with Life

70.

**Examining from
Multi-perspectives**

71.

Diverse Influences

72.

**Rising Above the Opinion of
Others**

73.

Release the Tyranny of the Mind

74.

The Graceful Pursuit of Understanding

75.

Expressing Feelings through Actions

76.

The Courage to Live Your Highest Truth

77.

Appreciative Awareness

78.

Guidance through Effortless Knowing

79.

Seeing the Best Possible

80.

Adventurous Perspective

81.

Sensitivity to the Nuances

82.

Trusting Your Better Judgment

83.

Spontaneous Innovation

84.

Self-reliant Support

85.

Releasing Blame

86.

Sensing New Opportunities

87.

Bridging Viewpoints through Communication

88.

Embracing the Unknowable

89.

Choosing a Heartfelt Path

90.

Cooperative Creations

91.

Playful Interactions

92.

Integrated Unity

93.

Increase through Emphases

94.

Graceful Journey

95.

**Empathic/Telepathic
Connection**

96.

**The Magic of Living in the
Moment**

Closing

The miraculous gifts of the Runes have not only come to restore and empower an ancient and sacred tradition, but have brought an unprecedented wealth of information: They have shed light on the inner psyche, the power of the acupressure points on the skin, and mapped the way to the evolved and glorious state of resurrection in unimaginable, illuminating ways.

The call has been issued to those who know that this sacred stewardship is for them; a call to walk a journey of holiness and mastery as a Rune Master upon the Earth.

Many have already heard the voice of the Runes in visions, dreams, and the soft whisperings of their heart. The mystery is calling, and although it is the ending of this book, it is just the beginning...

Appendix 1

Creating a Grand Master's Cloak

1. Measure from the neckline down, across the shoulder, down the arm and to the floor. That, plus approximately 6 inches, is the diameter of the cloak (if you want the front and back to drag a bit on the floor).

2. The runes (7 sets of 96) will be printed on the cloak as shown in the diagram. There will be 8 sheets of 12 runes for each set.

   Example: Set 1 is placed as follows
   1-12 is at the top (by the neckline) of 1a.

   Below that are runes 13-24, etc.
   The bottom of 1a will be runes 36-48.

   The top runes in column 1b will be runes 49-60.
   The bottom square of 1b will be runes 85-96.
   The other sets of runes will be similarly placed.

3. Only the rune sigils are used, not their interpretations.

4. Place a strong clasp, tie or braided closure at the neckline.

5. A hood may be attached per your preference.

6. The color of the cloak must be either black or forest green

A Grand Master's Cloak

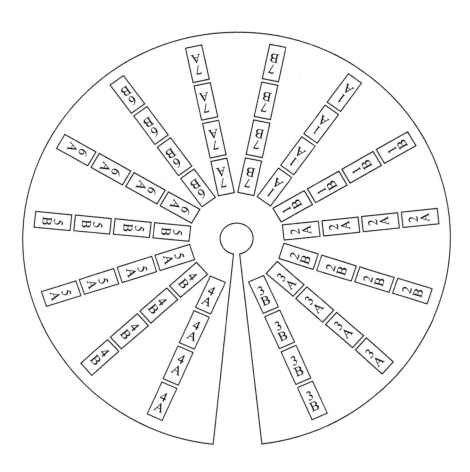

Recommended Handbooks for the Grand Master of the Runes

The Book of Runes
Understanding the Alchemy of the Runes

Alchemy is the science of transmutation: the adding of dissimilar components to create a leveraged result. In an alchemical equation, the sum total of the components is therefore much more than the parts added together.

The 672 runes found in this book are in a very specific order and each has a specific value. Every set forms an alchemical equation, and jointly they form a leveraged result. When the runes are added together into a combined book, the new powerful energy that turns the book into a power object is born.

"The power of this book will work, even if it is not read. The entire purpose of this book is: The full activation of the inner and outer senses, in order to dissolve the enslaving programs of belief systems." - The Seer Almine

ISBN Hardcover: 978-1-936926-96-1
Published 2015, color, 322 pages, hard cover, 8.5 x 11

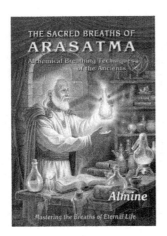

The Sacred Breaths of Arasatma
Alchemical Breathing Techniques of the Ancients

The Arasatma Breathing Technique was used by ancient mystics to activate the unused portion of the pranic tube for fuller self-expression and inner peace. A fully cleared and active pranic tube is the gateway to a magical life. Also, these breathing techniques aid in the restoration of the subtle, etheric functions of the body and senses. This allows the practitioner to access other dimensions and prolongs an eternal life of graceful unfolding. This book doesn't only share the first 3 levels of this powerful breathing technique but for the first time also publicly shares 3 follow-up levels to those who wish to continue their journey with this powerful transformative tool.

Published: 2013, 321 pages, 1:30 hours of meditational music
ISBN 978-1-936926-65-7

PDF download

CPSIA information can be obtained at www.ICGtesting.com
Printed in the USA
BVOW06s1033050416

443003BV00025B/267/P